BACK
TO
THE
BASICS

A COOKBOOK

BY

DESMOND
TAYLOR

First edition 1996

Text: © Desmond Taylor (1996)
Title photograph: © Wolfgang Stumpf (1996)

Published by ASPECTRA ®,
Layout: Wolfgang Stumpf,
Rua General Humberto Delgado Nº 5B, 8400 Lagoa, Algarve.
(No. Contribuinte 815 515 105)

Printed by Empresa Litográfica do Sul, S.A.,
Apartado 28, 8901 Vila Real de Santo António

Every reasonable care has been taken by the author and publishers in presenting the information in this book, but no responsibility can be taken for problems or claims arising from any inaccuracies.

ISBN: 972-97037-0-1   Depósito Legal: 102 875/96

Any suggestions from readers will be most gratefully received by the publishers.

FOREWORD

Most cookery books are a collection of recipes and may tend to be limited to a particular field. Whilst this book contains recipes it also covers the whole spectrum of cooking and aims at being a general kitchen reference book making for easier use of other cookery books.

Recipe books also tend to be written in one "language", using American, English / Imperial, or metric measures and using one form of oven temperatures. The "Useful Information" section gives equivalent tables and the recipes are in both Imperial and metric quantities with oven temperatures given in 3 ways.

Most cooks collect recipes from a variety of sources, try them and then modify them to their own taste or if a professional to the taste they feel their clientele will appreciate. It is probably true to say that it is rare for someone to create a completely new dish and there is no pretence that this collection contains any such rarity, but each recipe has been tried and met with approval from people who appreciate good food but who would not classify themselves as gourmets.

Each recipe has been based on 4 healthy portions.

CONTENTS

CONVERSION OF QUANTITIES, etc...

Most people tend to collect recipes from a variety of sources and a frequent problem is the different terminology used in various countries, it is hoped that the following tables will make easier to enjoy more international cooking.

	N. American	English	European
Butter	1 cup - 2 stick	8 oz.	225 g.
Cocoa	1 cup	4 oz.	112 g.
Flour	1 cup	4 oz.	112 g.
Rice	1 cup	8 oz.	225 g.
Rolled Oats	1 cup	2 ¾ oz.	75 g.
Sugar brown	1 cup	5 ¼ oz.	150 g.
Sugar gran	1 cup	8 oz.	225 g.
Sugar icing	1 cup	3 ¼oz.	90 g.
Breadcrumbs	1 cup	4 oz.	112 g.
Grated cheese	1 cup	4 oz.	112 g.
Cooked meat	1 cup	8 oz.	225 g.
Suet	1 cup	4 oz.	112 g.
Dried fruit	1 cup	5 oz.	112 g.
Liquids:	1 cup	8 fluid oz.	2 1/4 dl.

English recipes often use small measures in "spoons "

2 tablespoons butter = 1 oz. = 30 g. = 30 ml.
4 tablespoons flour = 1 oz. = 30 g. = 30 ml.
4 tablespoons cocoa = 1 oz. = 30 g. = 30 ml.

1 square of chocolate = 1 oz. = 30 g.

4 tablespoons liquid =1 wineglass = 60 ml. = 2 fluid oz.

WEIGHTS

ENGLISH		METRIC
1 tsp.		5 g.
1 tbsp.		15 g.
1 oz.		30 g.
2 oz.		60 g.
4 oz.	¼lb.	115 g.
8 oz.	½ lb.	225 g.
12 oz.	¾ lb.	340 g.
16 oz.	1 lb.	450 g.
32 oz.	2 lb.	900 g.
36 oz.	2 ¼lb.	1 kg.

LIQUID

	1 tsp.	5 ml	
	1 tbsp.	15 ml	
	2 tbsp.	30 ml	
¼ pint	5 fl. oz.	150 ml	
	8 fl. oz.	250 ml	¼ l
½ pint	10 fl. oz.	300 ml	
¾ pint	15 fl. oz.	425 ml	
	17 fl. oz.	500 ml	½ l.
1 pint	20 fl. oz.	575 ml	
1½ pint	30 fl. oz.	875 ml	
1¾ pint	35 fl. oz.	1000 ml	1 l.

CANS

In recipes can weights normally refer to the total contained weight,
i.e., including liquid .

7 oz.	200 g.
8 oz.	225 g.
10 oz.	250 g.
14 oz.	400 g.
15 oz.	425 g.
16 oz.	450 g.

OTHER EQUIVALENTS

3 lb. dressed chicken   when cooked = 2 ¼ lbs chopped meat
2 ½ lb. lobster   when cooked = 1 lb. meat
1 cup rice   when cooked = 3 cups

EQUIVALENT FOOD TERMS

English	American
Castor Sugar	Fine gran: (fruit) sugar
Demerara Sugar	Dark brown sugar
Treacle	Table Molasses
Black Treacle	Blackstrap
Corn flour	Cornstarch
Beetroot	Beet
Scones	Biscuit
Butter Muslin	Cheese cloth
Aubergine	Egg Plant
Jelly	Gelatine Dessert
Unsalted Butter	Sweet Butter
A vegetable resembling pumpkin or marrow	Squash

TEMPERATURE EQUIVALENTS

	Fahrenheit	Gas	Centigrade
Very slow	200-280	¼ - ½	115-135
Slow	280-320	1	135-160
Warm	320-340	3	160-170
Moderate	340-370	4	170-185
Fairly hot	370-400	5 - 6	185-205
Hot	400-440	7	205-225
Very hot	440-500	8 -9	225-250

SLOW COOK OR CROCKPOT COOKING

This is really a modernised version of casserole cooking in
a slow oven; there are many forms of crockpots on the
market but in general they have two settings,
high & low. The high setting generally conforms
to an oven of 150° C. / 300° F. / gas 3; the low
setting 120° C./ 200° F. / gas ½. Usually 1 hour
on high equals 2 hours on low.

There are two basic advantages for the crockpot; slow
cooking is a very useful technique for tenderising
poor quality meat and for allowing varying
flavours to infuse, secondly it is a very useful
tool for working housewives who can prepare
a meal and leave it slow cooking
while away from home.

A number of standard recipes can be adapted for the
slow cook pot, most of the casserole
dishes for example.

Where applicable the recipes contained in this book
gives the slow cook pot details.

SOUPS AND STARTERS

FRENCH ONION SOUP GRATINEE

450 g. / 1 lb. onions, thinly sliced
30 ml. / 2 tbsp. oil
15 g. / ½ oz. butter
10 ml. / 2 tsp. sugar
30 ml. / ½ oz. flour
900 ml. / 1½ pints beef stock
150 ml. / ¼ pint white wine
salt & pepper
pinch of ground nutmeg
50 ml. / 2 fl. oz. port or brandy

Croutons

8 slices French bread
olive oil
50 g. / 2 oz. grated cheese, preferably Gruyere

Gently sauté the onions in the oil and butter with the sugar. Cover and cook over low heat for 30 minutes or until tender and golden. Stir in the flour and cook for 2 minutes, add the stock, wine and seasonings and simmer for 30 minutes. Add the Port or brandy and continue to simmer for 15 minutes.

Meantime, make the croutons; put the bread on a baking tray and bake in a pre-heated oven at 80° C. / 350° F. / gas 4, until crisp and golden about 15 minutes, brush the toasted bread with oil.

Put the soup in bowls, put croutons on top, sprinkle with grated cheese and place under grill until bubbling and golden.

COCKIE - LEEKIE

1 kg. / 2 lb. stewing beef
1 boiling fowl
salt & pepper
1½ kg. / 3 lb. leeks
½ kg. / 1 lb. soaked prunes

Put beef in a pot big enough to hold the fowl later, bring to the boil and simmer for 30 minutes, skim, add the boiling fowl, seasoning and half the leeks, trimmed, cleaned left whole and tied in a bundle, Cover with water, cover and simmer until cooked, about 3 hours.

Remove beef and fowl, cut beef into cubes, strip meat from the fowl and cut into small pieces, return to the pot. About 20 minutes before serving remove leeks and discard, add the prunes and keep simmering.

About 5 minutes before serving add remaining leeks cleaned, trimmed and sliced.

CREAM OF TOMATO SOUP

½ kg. / 1 lb. ripe tomatoes
100 g. / 3 oz. chopped onions
125 g. / 4 oz. chopped carrot
bouquet garni
1 litre / 2 pints chicken stock
salt & pepper
300 ml. / ½ pint single cream
chopped basil

Simmer the vegetables and bouquet garni with ¾ of the stock until tender, remove the bouquet garni and purée the soup, add seasonings to taste and remaining stock. Bring cream to the boil in a clean pan and add the soup gradually; serve scattered with basil.

CREAM OF MUSHROOM SOUP

½ kg. / 1 lb. chopped field mushrooms
lemon juice
30 g. / 1 oz. chopped onion
60 g. / 2 oz. butter
clove of garlic
15 ml. / ¼ oz. flour
500 ml. / 1 pint chicken stock
150 ml. / ¼ pint single cream

Sprinkle the mushrooms with lemon juice. Sauté the onions in butter with the garlic, when soft stir in the mushrooms and the flour, cook gently for 2 minutes and then gradually add the stock.

When cooked purée, check seasonings and return to the pan, just before serving add the cream.

CHICKEN LIVER PATE

300 g. / 12 oz. chicken livers
30 ml. / 2 tbsp. Madeira
ground bay leaf
crushed clove of garlic
50 g. / 2 oz. white bread soaked in milk
100 g. / 4 oz. cooked ham chopped
200 g. / 8 oz. pork sausage meat
30 ml. / 2 tbsp. white wine
100 g. / 4 oz. streaky bacon

Wash the livers, marinate for 2 hours with the garlic, Madeira and bay leaf. Squeeze the bread dry and mince with the ham, sausage meat and livers, add the wine and leave mixture until soft.

Line an ovenware dish with the bacon and fill with the pate mixture, cover with foil and steam for 5 hours.

Cover with fresh foil and leave in refrigerator for several days to mature.

TUNA AND CORN CUPS

50 g. / 2 oz. butter
100 g. / 4 oz. white bread
200 g. / 8 oz. can of tuna steak
milk
200 g. / 8 oz. can sweet corn with red peppers
25 g. / 1 oz. flour
salt & pepper
sprigs of parsley for garnish

Melt half the butter in a small pan, brush 4 small pie tins with the butter, place a slice of bread without crusts, in each tin, brush with the rest of the melted butter, bake in a preheated oven 200° C., 400° F., gas 6, for 15 minutes.

Drain liquid from cans of tuna and corn, flake the tuna and make up the tuna liquid to 300 ml. / ½ pint with milk.

Melt the remaining butter in a pan, stir in the flour and cook gently for about 3 minutes, stir in the milk mixture and bring to the boil, cook for a further 3 minutes, then stir in the corn, tuna, salt and pepper.

Place the bread cups on individual warmed plates and spoon in the tuna/corn mixture garnish with the parsley and serve immediately.

SPRING ROLLS

The wrappers are better made in quantity and frozen for future use,
the quantity given makes 12 wrappers.

100 g. / 3 oz. flour
1 egg
a little milk
a pinch of salt

Sift flour and salt into a dough bowl, break in the egg and stir into a dough, a little milk may be necessary. Knead well, the more kneading the more elastic the dough will become, making the pastry thinner.

Roll out, making the pastry paper thin and transparent, but take care not to break it. Cut into 15 cm / 6 in. squares and cut each square into 2 triangular pieces. To freeze separate each piece with greaseproof paper. If using immediately cover with a damp cloth.

Filling
25 g. / 1 oz. minced pork lightly fried
2 dried Chinese mushrooms, soaked
2 canned water chestnuts, chopped
1 tsp. chopped fresh coriander leaves
1 spring onion, chopped
10 g. / ¼ oz. chopped bamboo shoot
a little grated carrot
10 g. / ¼ oz. beanshoots
10 g. / ¼ oz. raw shrimps
pinch of sugar
1 tsp. soya sauce
1 tsp. cornflour
pinch of salt
1 tbsp. oil

Drain mushrooms and shred together with onion; steep beansprouts in boiling water for a few minutes; peel and rinse shrimps, mix everything except oil and saute the mixture in hot oil for 2 or 3 minutes. Leave to cool.

Place a heaped tablespoon of the filling on a wrapper, turn in the 2 ends, fold over the last end and stick down with a little milk.

Deep fry until golden brown and crisp, serve with soya sauce. This is only one of many possible fillings and it pays to experiment.

BASIC PANCAKE BATTER

140 g. / 5 oz. plain flour
3 eggs
350 ml. / 12 fl. oz. milk
pinch of salt
butter to fry

Sift flour in a deep bowl, make a well in centre, break in the eggs and beat with whisk adding a little milk as necessary to form a thick batter; beat well to remove all lumps and then whisk in the rest of the milk. A mixer can be used.

Heat a nonstick pan for 2 or 3 minutes and then brush with a little butter, pour in a thin stream of batter from a jug, swirl it around in the pan so that it just covers thinly. Put pan on the heat and cook until golden brown at the edge and bubbling of the pan in the centre, then either flip the pancake over with a palette knife or be bold and "toss" it, cook the other side.

This quantity should make 20 pancakes, they can be frozen if layered with greaseproof paper.

These can be eaten in the traditional way sprinkled with sugar and lemon juice or used as wrappers with a variety of fillings for crepes.

PLAICE COUJONS

700 g. / ½ lb. plaice fillets skinned
75 g. / 3 oz. flour
salt and pepper
100 g. / 4 oz. dry bread crumbs
2 beaten eggs

Cut the fish on the diagonal into strips 6 mm. x 75 mm. / ¼ in. x 3 in.. Roll each strip in seasoned flour then in the egg and then in the bread crumbs. Chill for 1 hour, deep fry in hot oil for 30 seconds. Serve with Tartare sauce.

GARLIC MUSHROOMS

450 g. / 1 lb. small button mushrooms
40 g. / 1½ oz. butter
2 rashers of streaky bacon chopped
12 cloves of garlic, crushed
25 g. / 1 oz. bread crumbs
2 tbs. parsley finely chopped
salt and pepper
4 tbsp. lemon juice
lemon slices and parsley for garnish

Melt the butter in a pan and fry the mushrooms for 3 minutes until brown. Mix together the bacon, garlic, bread crumbs, parsley and seasoning and sprinkle over the mushrooms cook over a gentle heat stirring frequently for 10 minutes, add the lemon juice and adjust seasoning.

SCANDINAVIAN CABBAGE ROLLS

12 large cabbage leaves
1 beaten egg
59 ml. / 2 fl. oz. milk
50 g. / 2 oz. chopped onion
1 tsp. salt
1 tsp. pepper
450 g. / 1 lb. minced beef
225 g. / 8 oz. cooked rice
225 ml. / 8 fl. oz. tomato sauce
1 tbsp. brown sugar
1 tbsp. lemon juice
1 tsp. Worcestershire sauce

Immerse the cabbage leaves in large pan of boiling water until limp, about 3 minutes and drain well. Mix together the egg, milk, onion, salt, pepper, beef and cooked rice. Place about 50 g. / 2 oz. of the mixture in the centre of each leaf; fold in the sides and roll the ends over, place in an oven dish.

Mix the tomato sauce, sugar, lemon juice and Worcestershire sauce, pour over the cabbage leaves, cover the dish and cook in a low oven, 140° C. / 300° F. / gas 1 for 5 hours.

Slow cook pot: low 8 hours.

VEGETABLES

Cutting up vegetables

There are a number of standard terms used in recipes.

MIREPOIX   Coarsely chopped mixture of carrots, celery, onion, bacon or ham, parsley and thyme with a bay leaf. A mirepoix is always sieved out after cooking.

BRUNOISE   This usually consists of potatoes, carrots and tur nips, cut into thin slices then into tiny cubes; added to sauces which are not going to be sieved.

MACEDOINE   A mixture of carrots and turnips cut into ½cm / ¼ in. cubes, haricot beans cut across into cubes and peas.

DICE   Cut into 1 cm / ½ in. cubes

PAYSANNE   Carrots, turnips, potatoes sliced into ½ cm / ¼ in. slices, then cut into 1 cm / ½ in. squares. Used mainly for soups.

JULIENNE   Sliced thinly then cut into matchstick length strips.

ALLUMETTES
PAILLES   Usually potatoes sliced and cut to the size of match sticks.

CHIFFONADE   Leafy vegetables cut into shreds the width and length of a matchstick.

CHIPS   Root vegetables, usually potatoes cut into sticks 1 cm / ½ in. section about 5 cm / 2 in. long.

CAULIFLOWER AU GRATIN

Cook the cauliflower. Drain well keeping 300 ml. / ½ pt. of the liquid to make the Mornay sauce. While the sauce is simmering, break up the cauliflower into pieces and fry them lightly in butter, now mix in a little of the sauce.

Put a layer of the sauce into a gratin dish, spread the cauliflower on top and pour over the rest of the sauce. Sprinkle the top with 2 tbsp. of breadcrumbs and 1 tbsp. each of grated Parmesan and Gruyere, drip a little melted butter over the top and bake in oven 175° C./ 360° F. / gas 5 until top is golden brown.

The Mornay Sauce

2 tbsp. butter
1 chopped small onion
125 g. / 4 oz. chopped mushrooms
2 tbsp. flour
300 ml. / ½ pt. of the cooking liquid
300 ml. / ½ pt. milk
salt and pepper
90 g. / 3 oz. grated Gruyere
90 g. / 3 oz. grated Parmesan

Melt the butter and sauté the onion until soft, add the mushrooms, cover the pan and cook gently for 5 minutes; stir in the flour, then gradually add the stock followed by the milk and simmer down to a creamy consistency, check the seasoning.

Add the grated cheese and remove from the heat.

CARROTS AND ONIONS WITH APPLE

¾ kg. / 1½ lb. carrots
375 g. / 12 oz. sliced onions
60 g. / 2 oz. butter
375 g. / 12 oz. apples, peeled & sliced
salt & pepper,
7½ ml. / 1½ tsp. sugar
lemon juice

Cut the carrots into sticks and cook in lightly salted water with the sugar until almost tender. Fry the onions in butter until soft and golden but not brown, add them to the almost cooked carrots with the apples and complete the cooking.

Strain, add seasoning to suit and sprinkle with lemon juice to taste. Usually served with a pork dish.

GLAZED GINGER VEGETABLES

This is a different way of preparing ordinary vegetables for a special occasion, usually with uncooked beetroot, turnips, carrots etc., care must be taken to keep them separate to avoid colours and flavours mixing.

For 450 g. / 1 lb. of vegetable
12 g. / ½ oz. butter
22½ ml. / 1½ tbsp. sugar
salt
1 cm / ½ in. piece root ginger peeled and finely grated

Cut the vegetable into square sections about 3 cm / 1½ in. square and about 5 cm / 2 in. long, shave off the corners lengthways to achieve a barrel shape. Put all ingredients into a pan with just enough water to cover, bring to the boil swirling the liquid around, continue to boil vigorously until all liquid has gone, about 15-20 minutes. Vegetables should be tender and glazed, if still not tender add some boiling water and boil again to evaporation to obtain the glaze.

TIAN DE COURGETTES

450 g. / 1 lb. courgettes
salt
30 ml. / 2 tbsp. olive oil
2 thinly sliced onions
½ seeded & sliced red pepper in rings
½ seeded & sliced green pepper in rings
clove of garlic crushed
450 g / 1 lb. thinly sliced tomatoes
5 ml. / 1 tsp. sugar

2½ ml. / ½ tsp. each basil & oregano
salt & pepper
olive oil
45 ml. / 3 tbsp. breadcrumbs
45 ml. / 3 tbsp. grated Parmesan

Wash and dry the courgettes, slice thinly, sprinkle with plenty of salt and leave to sweat for 30 minutes, rinse in fresh water, drain and pat dry. Heat the oil in a heavy pan and saute the onion, peppers and garlic until soft and slightly brown.

Sprinkle the tomatoes with the sugar. Butter a gratin dish and cover the bottom with the onion/pepper mixture, arrange the tomatoes and courgettes in alternate overlapping layers across the dish, sprinkle with the herbs, season well, dribble over a little oil and bake in a pre-heated oven 180° C. / 350° F. /gas 4 for 30 minutes.

Sprinkle with breadcrumbs & cheese dribble a little more oil and continue to bake until top is crisp and golden.

COURGETTE ITALIENNE

450 g. / 1 lb. tomatoes
60 ml. / 4 tbsp. olive oil
2 thinly sliced small onions
2 cloves garlic, crushed
450 g. / 1 lb. courgettes, sliced
125 ml. / 4 fl. oz. chicken stock
5 ml. / 1 tsp. chopped fresh marjoram
salt & pepper
75 g. / 3 oz. caramelised roast almonds

Blanch the tomatoes quickly and remove the skins then quarter and seed. Heat the oil in a heavy pan and saute the onions and garlic, add courgettes and fry gently for 6-7 minutes stirring all the time, add the tomatoes and stock stir in marjoram and seasoning, cover and simmer gently until courgettes are tender, about 5 minutes. Quickly stir in the almonds and serve.

STUFFED COURGETTES

3 large courgettes
25 g. / 1 oz. lard
200 g. / ½ lb. minced beef
clove of garlic, crushed
15 ml. / 1 tbsp. tomato purée
10 ml. / 2 tsp. soya sauce
salt & pepper

Cut the courgettes in half lengthwise and scoop out the centre, chop up the flesh. Heat the oil in a pan and quickly brown the meat and garlic, stir in the purée, soya sauce and chopped flesh and season, spoon the mixture back into the courgette shells.

Place in a casserole dish carefully add a little water around them and put in a preheated oven 160° C. / 320° F. / gas 3 for 2½ hours.
Slow cook pot: Low 5-6 hours. High 2½-3 hours.

COURGETTES PROVENCALE

450 g. / 1 lb. courgettes, sliced thickly
450 g. / 1 lb. tomatoes, skinned & quartered
75 g. / 3 oz. grated Cheddar cheese
25 g. / 1 oz. butter
salt & pepper
pinch of dill seed

Layer the courgettes, tomatoes and cheese in a buttered casserole dish, seasoning each layer and ending with the cheese. Cook in a preheated oven 160° C. / 320° F. / gas 3 for 3 hours.
Slow cook pot: Low 5-6 hours. High 3 hours.

ONION BHAJIS

225 g. / 8 oz. flour
2 cloves garlic, crushed
pinch of salt
pinch of cummin
250 ml. / 9 fl. oz. milk
1 beaten egg
50 g. / 2 oz. butter
2 medium sliced onions
2 green chillies, sliced
oil

Put the flour, garlic, salt & cummin in a bowl and slowly beat in the milk and egg to make a batter. Melt the butter in a pan and cook the onions for a few minutes until soft, add the onions and chillies to the batter.

Heat the oil in a large pan and when hot add 1 heaped tbsp. of the batter, fry, turning until browned and cooked, remove with a slotted spoon and continue until all batter has been used.

Makes about 12.

Courgettes or mushrooms can be used instead of onions.

RATATOUILLE

50 g. / 2 oz. butter
1 sliced aubergine
2 thinly sliced medium onions
200 g. / ½ lb. sliced courgettes
1 clove garlic, crushed
salt & pepper
1 green pepper, seeded & sliced
200 g. / ½ lb. tomatoes, skinned & sliced

Melt half the butter in a pan & lightly fry the aubergine, onions and courgettes, add the garlic, remaining butter and season, cook for a few minutes, add the peppers and tomatoes check seasoning. Simmer gently for 2-3 hours, stir regularly. This dish can be cooked in a casserole in the oven on a very low heat 150° C. / 300° F. / gas 3 for 4 hours.

Slow cook pot: Low 8 hours. High 4 hours.

BRAISED CELERY

2 heads of celery
1 large diced onion
1 large diced carrot
50 g. / 2 oz. chopped bacon
25 g. / 1 oz. butter
salt & pepper
250 ml. / ½ pt. white or vegetable stock

Clean the celery and cut each stick in half and blanch in boiling water for 1 minute, drain. Fry the onion, carrot and bacon in the butter, put in the bottom of a casserole dish and season, place the celery on top and add the stock, cook in a preheated oven 150° C. / 300° F. / gas 3 for 2½ hours.
Slow cook pot: Low 6 hours. High 3 hours.
The celery may be served in the liquid or with a white sauce made from the liquid.

LEEK & MUSHROOM TART

Shortcrust pastry, 175 g. / 6 oz. flour
375 g. / 12 oz. leeks, sliced & halved
1 chopped medium onion
butter & oil
salt & pepper
125 g. / 4 oz. sliced mushrooms
1 egg
1 egg yolk
150 ml. / ¼ pt. single cream

Sauté the leeks and onions in a little butter and oil for about 10 minutes until soft, do not allow them to colour or become too wet, moist rather than wet. Cook the mushrooms in a separate pan in a little butter fairly rapidly for about 4 minutes. Add to the leek and season, leave to cool to tepid.
Line a 22 cm / 9 in. tart tin, with a removable base, with the pastry; beat together the egg, egg yolk, and cream, mix with the vegetables and spread over the pastry. Place in a preheated oven 190° C. / 375° F. / gas 5, for about 30 minutes, until filling is light brown on top and puffed up. Serve warm.

FRIED ONION RINGS

2 large Spanish onions
milk

Take the peeled onions and cut off the ends, these are not used, cut the remainder into slices about 3 mm / 1/8 in. thick; push out the rings discarding the small central piece. Soak the rings in salted milk for about 20 minutes; drain a few and shake them in a bag of seasoned flour and deep fry until crisp and brown, spread on absorbent paper and keep warm, until all are complete.

These go well with steak, chops or with vegetable dishes; instead of soaking in milk they can be dipped in batter before frying, this makes them heavier and more filling but just as good.

STUFFED MARROW

This will only be successful with a medium sized marrow, one that will fit into a large casserole dish.

Slice off the stalk end diagonally, hollow out the middle of the marrow with a long handled pointed, metal spoon. The finished result will look more attractive if long strips of peel are removed to give the outside a variegated appearance. Blanch the marrow in boiling salted water, making sure it is completely covered, for 4 minutes, drain well.

Now make a well spiced stuffing, one using rice rather than breadcrumbs, e.g. Greek Stuffing on p. 81.

Replace the stalk end which was sliced off and fix with a skewer, put the marrow into a pan, put some dots of butter on top and some basic tomato sauce round the sides, place in a preheated oven 180° C., 350° F., gas 4, for 1½ hours, basting occasionally then stir in the remainder of a pint of basic tomato sauce, and cook for a further 10 minutes.

POTATOES

It is assumed that everyone knows the normal ways of preparing boiled potatoes, of converting boiled potatoes into mashed, and of roasting in fat, and the family stand-by of deep fried chips; but there are a few alternative and relatively easy ways of having a change.

ROAST POTATOES

Prepare the potatoes and boil for 5 minutes in salted water, drain well, roll in flour and fry in hot oil for a few minutes until golden, put in a roasting dish in a preheated oven 200° C. / 400° F. / gas 6, for 40 minutes. This produces a crisp outside with a soft interior.
For the next three types of potato the same basic mixture is used:

500 g. / 1 lb. potatoes
2 egg yolks
25 g. / 1 oz. butter
salt & pepper

Boil the potatoes in the normal way until cooked, drain well and mash, return to the pan for a few moments to dry as much as possible, beat in the two egg yolks and season.

DUCHESSE POTATOES

Pipe the potato mixture into swirled cones on a greased baking sheet, brush with beaten egg, brown in a hot oven 220° C. / 420° F. / gas 7. Can also used in a nest shape to take such things as bean purée, etc.

CROQUETTE POTATOES

Soften the mixture with a little hot milk, then flavour; use chopped cob nuts or chopped parsley and chives, or grated Parmesan, or shrimps etc.; leave to get cold, form into croquette shapes dip in beaten egg, roll in breadcrumbs and fry in butter until golden brown all over.

POMMES DAUPHINE

First make a choux paste:

125 ml. / 4 fl. oz. water
¼ tsp. sugar
30 g. / 1 oz. butter
60 g. / 2 oz. plain flour
2 eggs
¼ tsp. salt

Boil the water, sugar and butter, stirring until the butter melts, remove from the heat, mix in the flour and return the pan to the heat for a few moments until the mixture leaves the side of the pan, remove and allow to cool for about 5 minutes. Beat in the eggs one at a time and the salt.

Now add this choux paste to the potato mixture, stirring to an even paste, then deep fry tablespoonfuls.

CORN FRITTERS

60 g. / 2 oz. plain flour
30 ml. /1 fl. oz. milk
pinch of both paprika & cayenne
1 egg yolk
¼ tsp. salt
175 g. / 6 oz. drained canned or cooked corn
1 egg white stiffly whipped

Mix the items in the order given and drop tablespoonfuls of the resulting batter into hot butter and fry until golden brown on both sides.

These are always served with Chicken Maryland but may used as a vegetable with other dishes.

FISH

Fish may be cooked in a variety of ways, but some ways are more suitable to particular fish than others.

FRYING

This is the most popular way of dealing with small fish cooked whole, fillets and cutlets.

After preparation the fish should be dried well; it must then be coated, this is essential, as fish must be fried in smoking hot fat a small quantity at a time, if the temperature of the fat drops too much it will be absorbed by the fish which becomes a greasy mess, but unless it is coated it will burn. The coating should also achieve a golden brown finish, after frying drain well on kitchen paper.

The coating can be:

Egg and breadcrumbs - Egg or milk and seasoned flour - Coating batter, page 90.

BAKING

This is probably the most suitable method for cooking whole fish possibly stuffed, but can also be used for steaks cut from a large fish and for small fish or fillets.

They can be prepared in a variety of ways, coated with egg and breadcrumbs, or brushed with melted butter, or sprinkled with lemon juice and white wine.

Preheated oven at 200° C. / 400° F. / gas 6
Whole fish 15-20 minutes per lb.
Thick steaks 15-20 minutes.
Small fish and fillets 10-15 minutes.
Serve with lemon slices and a sauce

GRILLING

This is an ideal method for oily fish such as mackerel and sardines but is also useful for herrings, mullet, sole and plaice, it may also be very successful with steaks of thick fish such as salmon, halibut and cod.

The grill pan should be greased to prevent the fish from sticking; sprinkle the fish with lemon juice and dot with butter, place under a hot grill and cook until light brown, fillets only need cooking on the flesh side for about 5 minutes, whole fish need browning on both sides, steaks about 35 cm / 1½ in. thick will need about 10 minutes each side.

Maître d'hôtel butter goes well with grilled fish, but always serve with lemon slices and if not the butter some other sauce.

POACHING

This is usually reserved for smoked haddock or kippers. It is best to use a frying pan to allow the whole fish to lay flat, half fill the pan with water and bring to the boil, add the fish and simmer very gently until cooked i.e., when the flesh easily leaves the bone, about 15 minutes per 400 g. / lb.

STEAMING

This is the usual method of preparation for children and invalids, normally white fish is used, and it can be whole fish, fillets or steaks. Sprinkle with lemon juice, salt and pepper.

Whole fish need 15-20 minutes per 400 g. / lb., fillets and steaks about 15 minutes but when cooked the flesh will leave the bone easily.

Serve with lemon slices and a sauce.

FORCEMEAT STUFFING FOR FISH

100 g. / 3 oz. breadcrumbs
25 g. / 1 oz. suet or melted margarine
grated rind of ½ lemon
2½ ml. / ½ tsp. dried herbs
10 ml. / 2 tsp. chopped parsley
salt & pepper
1 beaten egg

Mix all the ingredients together adding sufficient beaten egg to bind the mixture. This is a regularly used stuffing for baked fish.

BAKED STUFFED SOLE

Take 1 large sole, trim, make a cut down the centre back and loosen the flesh close to the bone on each side; stuff with fish forcemeat and put on a greased baking tray, cover with greased paper, and cook for 20-30 minutes at 200° C. / 400° F. / gas 6.

Serve with lemon slices and sliced cucumber

BAKED FISH STEAKS

6 fish steaks
fish forcemeat
30 g. / 1 oz. butter
30 ml. / 2 tbsp. milk
tomatoes

Stuff the steaks with the forcemeat, place in a greased oven dish, put a little butter on each one, pour the milk around and cover with greaseproof paper, bake for 25 minutes at 200° C. / 400° F. / gas 6. After 15 minutes cut the tomatoes in half add put in the oven.

Serve the fish with the tomatoes, lemon slices and a sauce.

SOUSED HERRINGS

4 herrings
salt, pepper & bay leaf
Tarragon vinegar & water

Clean and scale the fish, remove the roe, cut down the front and remove the backbone, season with salt and pepper and put a small piece of bay leaf on each.

Roll up the fish and pack fairly tightly in an oven dish, cover with equal quantities of the vinegar and water.

Bake for 1 hour at 170° C. / 350° F. / gas 3, allow to cool and serve in the liquid.

HALIBUT WITH BECHAMEL SAUCE

700 g. / 1½ lb. halibut
50 g. / 2 oz. melted butter
350 ml. / 12 fl. oz. Bechamel sauce (page 71)
salt & pepper
10 ml. / 2 tsp. lemon juice
few drops of onion juice
2 hard boiled eggs

Clean the fish and cut into 8 fillets, add the seasonings to the melted butter, dip each fillet into the butter, roll up, fasten with a wooden skewer.

Put into an oven dish, dredge with flour and bake for 12 minutes at 200° C. / 400° F. / gas 6. Put onto a serving dish, pour around the sauce and garnish with the chopped hard boiled eggs.

DOVER SOLE WITH LEMON SAUCE

4 fillets of sole
15 g. / ½ oz. butter
30 g. / 1 oz. flour
150 ml. / ¼ pt. milk
150 ml. / ¼ pt. fish stock
1 egg
juice of 1 lemon
7½ ml. / 1½ tsp. sugar

Bake or grill the sole. Melt the butter and blend in the flour with a little milk, gradually blend in the rest of the milk and the fish stock and bring to the boil, cook for 2-3 minutes, add the egg and cook for a further 2 minutes; but do not boil. Stir in the lemon juice, sugar and seasoning.

Serve the sauce hot with the fish.

BAKED DRESSED TROUT

1 kg. / 2 lbs. trout fillets
Lime or lemon juice
250 g. / 10 oz. can of mushroom pieces
30 g / 1 oz. butter
30 g. / 1 oz. chopped onion
15 g. / ½ oz. flour
200 ml. / 6 fl. oz. cream
pinch thyme
1 chopped tomato
salt & pepper
chopped parsley

Cut the fillets into 6 pieces, sprinkle with the fruit juice and let stand for ½ hour. Drain the mushrooms saving the liquid. Saute the onion in butter for 1 or 2 minutes, blend in the flour and the mushroom liquid, cook and stir until very thick, add the mushrooms, cream and thyme. Remove from the heat, add the tomato and season to taste. Lightly grease 6 baking foil squares and place a piece of trout on each, top with the mushroom mixture, sprinkle with parsley and wrap airtight. Bake on an oven sheet for 20 minutes. 210° C., 425° F., gas 7. Serve with a little hot lemon butter sauce.

BAKED TROUT IN RED WINE

4 trout - one per person
2 medium chopped onions
2 medium chopped carrots
Little butter
Red wine
39 g. / 1 oz. flour
30 g. / 1 oz. butter
30 g. / 1 oz. butter

Lightly cook the onion and carrot in a little butter and put in a heatproof dish. Clean and dry the trout, season inside and out, put in the dish and nearly cover the trout with red wine, (the dish should just contain the fish).
Start cooking on top of stove until simmering then place in a hot

oven, 200° C. / 400° F. / gas 7 for 10 minutes, drain off the cooking juices into a separate pan and strain.

Melt 1 oz. of butter and blend in the flour, gradually add the strained cooking juices and blend well, cook for 1 minute, then add the second 1 oz. of butter.

Serve the trout with the hot wine sauce.

SALMON TROUT IN WHITE WINE

1 small salmon trout - 1¼ Kg. / 2½ lbs.
salt & pepper
350 g. / ¾ lbs. mushrooms
350 ml. / 12 fl. oz. dry white wine
1 lemon
50 g. / 2 oz. butter
30 g. / 1 oz. duxelles
225 g. / ½ lb. tomatoes

Clean the fish , cut off the head, season well and place in an oven-proof dish, surround with the sliced mushrooms, pour over the wine and the juice of the lemon; dot with small pieces of butter.

Cover and cook in a preheated oven 180° C. / 350° F. / gas 4 for 30 minutes. Pour off the juices into a separate pan add the duxelles and thinly sliced tomatoes, warm the sauce and pour over the fish.

CHEESE AND FISH PIE

750 g. / 1½ lbs. potatoes, mashed
100 g. / 4 oz. grated cheese
500 g. / 1 lb. cooked white fish
450 ml. / ¾ pt. white sauce - medium (page 73)
20 ml. / ¾ oz. chopped parsley
salt & pepper
lemon slices for garnish

Mix the potato and cheese, line a greased pie dish with the mixture retaining enough to cover the top. Mix the flaked cooked fish, sauce, parsley and seasoning to taste, put in the dish and cover with the rest of the potato mixture.

Bake in a preheated oven 190° C. / 375° F. / gas 5 for 40 minutes. Serve garnished with lemon slices.

SAVOURY FISH PASTIES

350 g. / 12 oz. short crust pastry
225 g. / 8 oz. cooked fish (haddock is very good)
15 g. / ½ oz. butter
15 g. / ½ oz. flour
150 ml. / ¼ pt. milk
salt & pepper
15 g. / 3 tsp. capers
2 sliced hard-boiled eggs
2 sliced tomatoes

Roll out the pastry into 4 large squares about 5 mm / ¼ in. thick. Make a sauce with the butter, flour and milk, season well and add the flaked fish, capers, eggs and tomatoes put the mixture in the centre of each pastry square, brush the edges of the pastry with milk and bring the corners to the centre making an envelope, press the edges together firmly.

Put onto a greased baking tray and brush with beaten egg and bake in a preheated oven for 25 minutes at 230° C. / 450° F. / gas 8. Reduce heat to 200° C. / 400° F. / gas 6 for a further 10 minutes. Serve hot or cold.

MEAT & POULTRY

Cuts of meat:

Unfortunately for people who like to collect recipes from various countries we find that different places butcher their animals in different ways, so that a recipe will call for a cut or joint which is not available in our country.

The basic methods are: American, English, and Continental (French); to help the adventurous each section starts with a diagram showing each method with the various cuts named, except for the Continental as each country has its own name for them.

METHODS OF COOKING

ROASTING

This is really only suitable for fair-sized joints of top quality meat. There are two ways; always use a preheated oven:

Cook rapidly at 220° C. / 425° F, gas 7, for 20 to 30 minutes, then reduce the heat 190° C. / 315° F. / gas 5, for the rest of the time. Or, cook for the calculated time plus a third, at 175° C. / 350° F. / gas 4. Calculated time:
Beef and Mutton: thin joints 15 minutes per ½ Kg. / 1 lb., plus 15 minutes.
Thick joints: 20-25 minutes per ½ Kg. / 1 lb., plus 20-25 minutes.
Veal and Pork: 25-30 minutes per ½ Kg. / 1 lb. plus 25-30 minutes, never serve underdone

BRAISING

This is a combination of roasting and stewing, and may be done in the oven in a casserole or covered ovendish, or in a heavy bottomed stewpan on the top of the stove. The meat is cooked on a bed of vegetables cut into chunks which are lightly fried before putting in the pot, the meat is also lightly browned before adding on top . Nearly cover with sufficient hot stock simmer gently on top of stove or in a moderate oven 175° C. / 350° F. / gas 4, basting every 30 minutes.
Cooking time:
Joints suitable for roasting allow half as long again as for roasting.

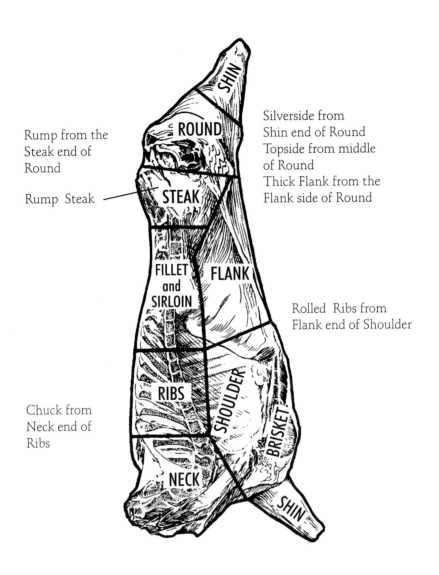

Rump from the
Steak end of
Round

Rump Steak

Silverside from
Shin end of Round
Topside from middle
of Round
Thick Flank from the
Flank side of Round

Rolled Ribs from
Flank end of Shoulder

Chuck from
Neck end of
Ribs

SHIN

ROUND

STEAK

FILLET
and
SIRLOIN

FLANK

RIBS

SHOULDER

BRISKET

NECK

SHIN

ENGLISH CUTS OF BEEF

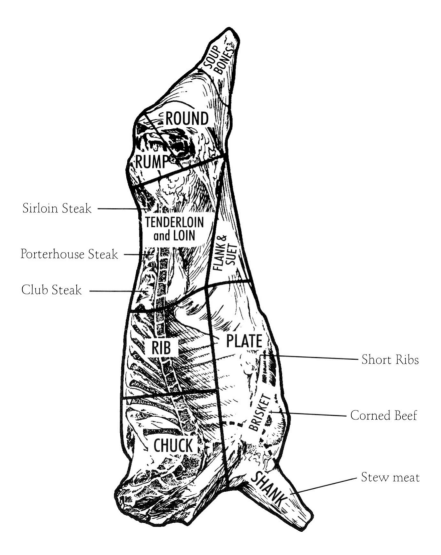

SOUP BONES

ROUND

RUMP

Sirloin Steak

TENDERLOIN and LOIN

Porterhouse Steak

FLANK & SUET

Club Steak

RIB

PLATE

Short Ribs

BRISKET

Corned Beef

CHUCK

SHANK

Stew meat

AMERICAN CUTS OF BEEF

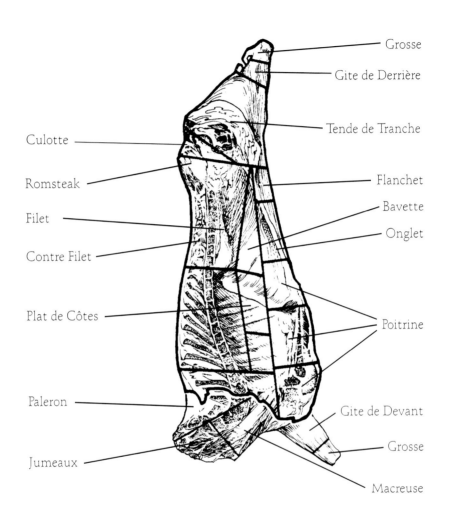

Grosse

Gite de Derrière

Tende de Tranche

Culotte

Flanchet

Romsteak

Bavette

Filet

Onglet

Contre Filet

Plat de Côtes

Poitrine

Paleron

Gite de Devant

Grosse

Jumeaux

Macreuse

CONTINENTAL CUTS OF BEEF

Stewing meat - 3 hours.
Rabbit - 1 to 2 hours.
Chicken - 1 hour.
Boiling fowl - 2 hours.

GRILLING

This method can only be used for small tender cuts of meat, chops, steaks, calves liver, kidneys etc. Always lightly season the meat and brush with melted fat before placing on a hot greased grid .

Cooking time:
Steak 4 cm. : 1½ in. thick; 12-15 minutes.
Lamb chops : 8-10 minutes.
Pork chops : 15-20 minutes.
Veal cutlets : 15-20 minutes.
Liver : 10 minutes.
Kidneys : 10 minutes.
Sausages : 10-15 minutes.

OXTAIL STEW

1 kg. / 2 lbs. oxtail, cut in 5 cm / 2 in. lengths
30 g. / 1 oz. flour
salt &pepper
1 tbsp. oil
1 small tomato, peeled & chopped
1 small onion, chopped
2 carrots, chopped
1 turnip, chopped
1 crushed clove garlic
small bay leaf
350 ml. / 12 fl. oz. beef stock
125 ml. / 4 fl. oz. port
leek, sliced

Coat the meat in the seasoned flour, heat the oil in a large frying pan and brown the meat. Put all the ingredients in a large stew pot, cover and cook, gently simmering for 5 or 6 hours, until the meat comes easily off the bone.

Remove the meat and bay leaf, take the meat off the bones, dice and return to the pot, let it stand for a few minutes and skim off the excess fat.

Slow cook pot: this is an excellent way to prepare this dish; cook on Low for 7 or 8 hours.

LASAGNE

150 g. / 6 oz. minced beef
100 g. / 4 oz. minced pork
1 small chopped onion
200 g. / 8 oz. can tomatoes, chopped
100 ml. / 4 fl. oz. tomato sauce
1 beef stock cube crushed
1 tsp. dried parsley
1 tsp. sugar
pinch of salt & rubbed basil
200 g. / 8 oz. cottage cheese
50 g. / 1 oz. grated Parmesan cheese
pinch of salt & rubbed oregano
100 g. / 4 oz. lasagne noodles, cooked & drained
100 g. / 4 oz. mozzarella cheese, sliced

In a large frying pan melt a little butter and cook the beef, pork, onion and a little crushed garlic to taste, then drain of excess fat. Mix the meat with the tomatoes, tomato sauce, beef cube, parsley, sugar, salt and basil, cover and cook slowly in preheated oven for 3 hours. 150° C. / 200° F. / gas 3.

Mix together the cottage cheese, half the Parmesan, the salt and oregano.

Take an oven dish about 15 cm × 10 cm / 7 in. × 4½ in., grease it lightly with butter, layer half the noodles, the meat mixture, the mozzarella cheese and the cottage cheese mix, repeat this layer but reserving enough of the meat mixture to put on the top, sprinkle with the remaining half of the Parmesan and cook in preheated oven 175° C. / 350° F. / gas 5 for 45 minutes.

CHUCK ROAST

1 kg. / 2 lb. chuck roasting joint
salt & pepper
2 small onions cut in quarters
4 small carrots cut in quarters
1 stalk of celery, cut in cubes
1 bay leaf
2 tbsp. vinegar
1 l. / 1¾ pt. water
1 small cabbage, cut in chunks

Rub the meat well with the seasonings; put the onions, carrots and celery in an oven dish place the meat on top, add the bay leaf, vinegar and water, cover the dish and cook in a preheated oven 150° C. / 300° F. / gas 3 for about 2 hours, or until meat is tender; remove meat, put the cabbage in the dish, turn up heat and cook until done, about 20 minutes; keep the meat warm. Meanwhile make the sauce.

Sauce

45 g. / 1½ oz. butter
15 g. / ½ oz. flour
15 g. / ½ oz. finely chopped onion
350 ml. / 12 fl. oz. of the cooking liquid
30 g. / 1 oz. prepared horseradish
pinch of salt

Melt the butter in a saucepan, stir in flour and onion over low heat to make a roux, gradually add the liquid, blending thoroughly, add the horseradish and salt, cook over low heat until thickened and smooth. Drain the vegetables from the dish and serve with the meat and sauce.

BOILED BEEF AND DUMPLINGS

1 kg. / 2 lb. Silverside or brisket of beef
1 medium sliced onion
3 medium sliced carrots
salt & pepper
500 ml. / 1 pt. boiling water

Put meat and vegetables into a stew pan with the .seasoning and boiling water bring to the boil and simmer for 4 to 5 hours. ½ hour before serving add the dumplings.

Dumplings:

100 g. / 4 oz. flour
50 g. / 2 oz. shredded suet
salt & pepper
water to mix

Mix together the flour, suet and seasoning with sufficient water to bind; mould into balls and drop in in the simmering stew.

BEEF STEW

¾ kg. / 1 ½ lbs. stewing beef, cubed
flour
1 bay leaf
1 tbsp. Worcestershire sauce
1 chopped onion
200 ml. / 7 fl. oz. beef stock
salt & pepper
4 sliced carrots
150 g. / 5 oz. sliced celery
3 potatoes cubed
10 small onions
1 medium turnip, cubed
570 ml. / 1 pt. water

Roll the meat in the flour and brown in hot oil in a frying pan, put the meat and all the ingredients into a stew pan, bring to the boil and simmer gently for 5 hours, thicken as necessary with flour. Dumplings may be added.

Slow cook pot: Low for 8 hours.

OX TONGUE

1 - 1½ kg. / 2½ - 3 lb. ox tongue
1 medium sliced onion
bouquet garni
2 tsp. vinegar or lemon juice
few peppercorns
250 ml. / ½ pt. boiling water

Put all the ingredients in a stewpan, bring to the boil and simmer gently for about 5 hours. When cooked, remove the skin and any small bones, roll the tongue and put into a tight fitting cake tin.

Boil the cooking liquid rapidly for 3-4 minutes to reduce it, pour over the tongue, put a loose fitting plate on the top and a heavy weight on top.

Leave to go cold and set, then turn out of the tin.

Slow cook pot: This recipe is ideal for the cook pot, High for 6-7 hours.

STEAK DIANE

4 fillet steaks
100 g. / 4 oz. butter
1 small onion, finely chopped
75 g. / 3 oz. sliced mushrooms
salt & pepper
1 tbsp. lemon juice
2 tbsp. worcestershire sauce
pinch of sugar
4 tsp. brandy
chopped parsley

Melt half the butter in a frying pan and saute the onion until soft, remove from the pan and keep warm, turn up the heat and fry the steaks for 1-2 minutes each side until lightly browned.

Add the rest of the butter and mushrooms; return the onions to the pan, stir well and season. Pour in the lemon juice and sauce, sprinkle in the sugar and bring to the boil.

Pour in the brandy and ignite, let the flames die out before stirring in the parsley.

WALNUT MEAT LOAF

½ kg. / 1 lb. minced beef
1 beaten egg
30 ml. / 1 fl. oz. milk
1 tsp. worcestershire sauce
1 tbsp. finely chopped onion
salt & pepper
60 ml. / 2 fl. oz. tomato sauce
30 ml. / 1 fl. oz. water

Mix all together except water and sauce, flatten out on waxed paper in rectangular shape about 2 cm / ¾ inches thick.

Stuffing

150 g. / 6 oz. soft bread crumbs
1 tbsp. finely chopped onion
salt & pepper
150 g. / 6 oz. chopped celery
60 ml. / 2 fl. oz. milk
100 g. / 4 oz. chopped walnuts

Mix together and shape into a roll on top of the meat, roll up the meat so that it covers the stuffing, now remove the waxed paper.

Place the meat roll in a shallow baking dish and pour over the mixed water and tomato sauce, bake in a preheated oven for 1½ hours at 190° C. / 375° F. / gas 5.

Garnish with orange slices and toasted walnuts.

SIRLOIN STEAK WITH WHISKY SAUCE

1 kg. / 2 lb. sirloin steak
90 ml. / 3 fl. oz. whisky
150 ml. / ¼ pt. beef stock
2 tsp. green peppercorns
150 ml. / ¼ pt. double cream
salt & pepper

Cut the meat into 4 steaks, brush a frying pan with oil and put over a high heat until it smokes, put the steaks in the pan and fry for 3 minutes each side, lift them every now and again to prevent them sticking.

Spoon the whisky over the steaks and cook for a few minutes, take them out of the pan and keep warm. Put the stock, cream and peppercorns in the pan, season and simmer for a few minutes stirring continuously, stir any juices that have come out of the steaks into the sauce.

Pour the sauce over the steaks and serve.

BEEF OLIVES

1 kg. / 2 lb. topside of beef
450 g. / 1 lb. minced veal
1 small onion, grated
1 tbsp. chopped parsley
pinch of grated nutmeg
salt & pepper
1 large sliced onion
1 large chopped carrot
1 tbsp. flour
300 ml. / ½pt. beef stock
300 ml. / ½ pt. red wine
bouquet garni
225 g. / ½ lb. button mushrooms

Cut the beef into very thin slices and flatten. Make the stuffing by mixing the veal, grated onion, parsley, nutmeg and seasoning. Put the stuffing on each slice of beef, then roll up the slices and secure with a toothpick.

Heat a little oil in a frying pan and brown the beef rolls, put them into a casserole, add the sliced onion and carrot to the frying pan and brown them a little before putting them in the casserole. Sprinkle the flour into the pan juices and stir it in, slowly add the stock and stir into a smooth sauce, add the wine and season, pour over beef rolls and add the bouquet garni; cover and cook in a preheated oven for 2 hours at 150° C. / 300° F. / gas 2.

Take the rolls out of the casserole and remove the toothpicks, return the rolls to the pot and add the mushrooms, cook for another 30 minutes.

These olives are also known as rolls, birds or paupiettes; pork tenderloin, veal or turkey can be used instead of beef.

BEEF BOURGUIGNONNE
BŒUF A LA BOURGUIGNONNE

1 kg. / 2 lb. stewing beef
225 g. / ½ lb. button onions
110 g. / ¼ lb. streaky bacon
2 tbsp. flour
salt & pepper
pinch of marjoram and thyme
175 ml. / 6 fl. oz. beef stock
350 ml. / 12 fl. oz. red wine
225 g. / ½ lb. button mushrooms

Fry the onions whole with the diced bacon in a little oil until brown, then transfer to a casserole dish. Cut the meat into cubes and lightly brown in the pan, sprinkle with the flour and the seasonings, stir well and put in the casserole. Bring the stock and wine to the boil in the pan and pour into the casserole, cover and cook in a preheated oven for 3 hours at 150° C./ 300° F. / gas 2. Add the mushrooms and cook for another 30 minutes.

If more liquid is needed during the cooking add more stock and wine in the original proportions.

BŒUF A L' ANCIENNE

This is probably the original beef bourguignonne recipe.

1 kg. / 2 lb. stewing beef
225 g. / ½ lb. sliced carrots
1 large sliced onion
2 tsp. dried thyme
2 bay leaves, crumbled
2 tbsp. chopped parsley
2 cloves garlic, crushed
2 chopped shallots
225 g. / ½ lb. finely sliced mushrooms
salt & pepper
45 ml. / 1½ fl. oz. brandy
600 ml. / 1 pt. dry Madeira wine
75 g. / 3 oz. sliced streaky bacon

Cut the meat into cubes. Use a small casserole, put a layer of carrots and onions on the bottom of the pot and sprinkle with some thyme, bay leaf and parsley: place on a layer of beef, put on some garlic, more onion and shallots, then some mushrooms.

Continue layering until all the meat is used, season each layer well with salt and pepper; pour over the brandy and Madeira and place the slices of bacon on top.

Bring the pot to the boil on top of the stove then cover with a tight fitting lid and cook in a preheated oven for 6 hours at 140 C. / 275 F. / gas 1. **DO NOT LIFT THE LID.**

Slow cook pot: This is obviously an ideal dish for a slow cook pot. Low for 8 hours.

BEEF STROGANOFF

1 kg. / 2 lb. rump or fillet steak
fresh ground black pepper
30 g. / 1 oz. finely chopped onion
60 g. / 2 oz. butter
225 g. / ½ lb. sliced button mushrooms
salt, nutmeg and mace
300 ml. / ½ pt. sour cream

Cut the steak across the grain into slices 1 cm / ½ in. thick, season with the black pepper and flatten. Saute the onion in half the butter until golden, add the steak and saute for 5 minutes.

Remove from the pan and keep warm. Add the remaining butter to the pan and cook the mushrooms. Return the beef to the pan and season to taste with salt, nutmeg and mace, add the cream and heat through.

CHILLI CON CARNE

725 g. / 1½ lb. beef, finely chopped **NOT** minced
1 large chopped onion
3 cloves garlic, crushed
1 small green pepper, seeded and sliced
2 chopped sticks celery
2 tsp. chilli powder
425 g./ 15 oz. tin tomatoes
425 g. / 15 oz. tin red beans, drained
salt

Brown the meat in a little oil in a frying pan. Put the meat in a casserole dish with all the other ingredients, cover and cook in a pre-heated oven for 3-4 hours at 150 C. / 300 F. / gas 3

Slow cook pot: Low for 6-8 hours. High for 3-4 hours.

BEEF WELLINGTON

1 kg. / 2½ lb. whole fillet of beef
30 g. / 1 oz. softened butter
salt & pepper
60 g. / 2 oz. diced celery
60 g. / 2 oz. diced onion
60 g. / 2 oz. diced carrot
1 tsp. rosemary
30 g. / 1 oz. chopped parsley
60 ml. / 2 fl. oz. red wine
chicken liver pate
225 g. / 8 oz. shortcrust pastry
1 beaten egg yolk

120 ml. / 4 fl. oz. chicken stock
30 g. / 1 oz. extra pate
60 g. / 2 oz. sliced mushrooms

Spread the butter over the whole surface of the beef, sprinkle with salt and pepper, put the vegetables in a roasting dish with the herbs, pour over the red wine, place the meat on top and roast in a preheated oven for 1 hour at 230° C. / 450° F. / gas 8, turn the meat several times. Remove the roast and cool thoroughly, it can be kept in the refrigerator overnight.

When completely cold, cover the whole surface of the meat with the pate about ½ cm. / ¼ in. thick Roll out the pastry about ¼ cm. / 1/8 in. thick and wrap around the meat, sealing well; brush with beaten egg. Lay on a greased baking tray and bake in a preheated oven for about 25 minutes until crust is well browned, at 210 C. / 425 F. / gas 7.

Puree the vegetables from the roasting pan and replace in the pan, add the stock, pate and mushrooms and simmer for 15 minutes.
Slice the meat with a very sharp knife and serve with the hot sauce.

BRAISED LAMB WITH VEGETABLES

1 kg. / 2 lb. stewing lamb
flour
2 tbsp. fat, bacon dripping preferred
250 ml. / 8 fl. oz. chicken stock
1 sliced onion
250 g. / 10 oz. tin of tomatoes
1 clove
salt & pepper
pinch of tarragon and thyme
6 small scraped carrots
6 small scraped potatoes
180 g. / 6 oz. button mushrooms
180 g. / 6 oz. cut green beans
1 tbsp. butter
1 tbsp. flour

Cut the meat into serving slices, dust with flour and brown the meat slowly in the hot fat in a deep saucepan. Drain off the fat and add the stock to the pan stirring to dissolve any brown bits, now add the

The leg may be divided
into two parts:
Fillet of leg and the
Shank end.

Chump chop from
the leg end of loin

Lamb cutlet from
the best end of neck

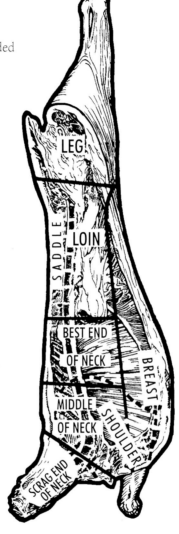

ENGLISH CUTS OF MUTTON

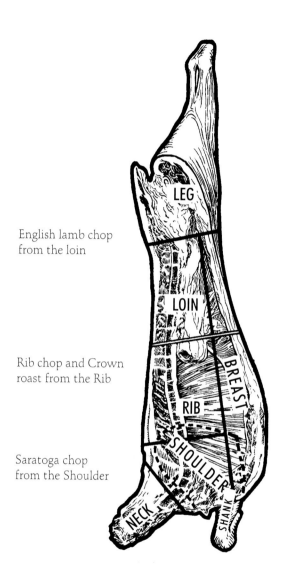

English lamb chop
from the loin

Rib chop and Crown
roast from the Rib

Saratoga chop
from the Shoulder

AMERICAN CUTS OF MUTTON

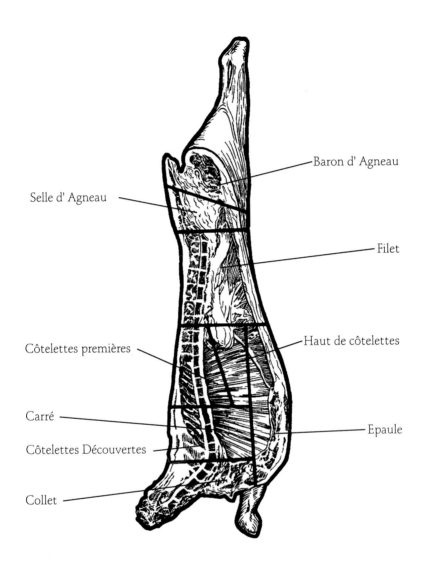

Baron d' Agneau

Selle d' Agneau

Filet

Côtelettes premières

Haut de côtelettes

Carré

Epaule

Côtelettes Découvertes

Collet

CONTINENTAL CUTS OF MUTTON

tomatoes and herbs; cover the pan and simmer for 1 hour.

Now add the vegetables and continue to simmer until they are tender. Strain the liquid into a small saucepan add the creamed together flour and butter and cook until thickened, pour over the meat and vegetables, reheat and serve sprinkled with parsley.

STUFFED BREAST OF LAMB

1 kg. / 2 lb. breast of lamb, boned and trimmed
2 tbsp. oil
175 g. / 6 oz. sausagemeat
2 tbsp. port
2 tbsp. chopped parsley
grated rind of ½ lemon
100 g. / 4 oz. cooked leaf spinach
pinch of ground nutmeg
salt & pepper
100 g. / 4 oz. dried apricots

Soak the apricots overnight.

Blend the sausagemeat, port, parsley, lemon rind, spinach, nutmeg and seasoning in a mixer until smooth.

Lay the meat flat and spread the stuffing mixture evenly all over, roll the breast up loosely and secure with string.

Preheat the oven to 180° C. / 350° F. / gas 4, heat the oil in a roasting dish and place the joint in it, cook for 1½ hours, basting occasionally until golden brown.

Put the apricots with the water in which they had soaked, about 600 ml. / 1 pt. into a mixer and blend until smooth, pour into a saucepan, add any cooking juices from the roasting pan, heat thoroughly, season and serve with the lamb.

BRAISED ORANGE LAMB

1 shoulder of lamb, boned, flattened 1 kg. / 2 lb.
100 g. / 4 oz. white breadcrumbs
50 g. / 2 oz. seedless raisins
50 g. / 2 oz. shredded suet
large pinch of majoram
salt & pepper

2 large oranges
1 beaten egg
30 g. / 1 oz. lard
125 ml / ¼ pt. brown stock
2 tbsp. red wine
2 tbsp. redcurrant jelly

Mix together breadcrumbs, raisins, suet, seasoning and grated rind of the oranges and bind together with the beaten egg.

Spread this stuffing evenly over the lamb, roll up and tie with string. Heat the lard in a frying pan and brown the joint all over.

Remove the pith from the oranges slice thickly and place in the bottom of a casserole dish, place the drained joint on top, pour over the stock and wine and cook in a preheated oven for 5 hours at 150 C. / 300 F. / gas 3. Just before serving stir in the redcurrant jelly.

Slow cook pot: High for 5-6 hours.

IRISH STEW

1 kg. / 2 lb. lamb, cubed
Salt & pepper
700 ml. / 1¼ pt. beef stock
2 sliced carrots
2 sliced onions
4 potatoes quartered
1 bay leaf
¼ tsp. majoram
¼ tsp. thyme
150 g. / 5 oz. peas
30 g. / 1 oz. flour
30 g. / 1 oz. butter

Heat a little oil in a frying pan and brown the lamb . Put the meat and all the other ingredients, except peas, flour and butter, in a stew pan, bring to the boil and simmer gently for 4-5 hours. Add the peas ½ hour. before serving. Just before serving thicken with the flour and butter.

Slow cook pot: This is an excellent dish for a cook pot; Low for 10 hours., turn to High for the thickening.

LAMB PROVENÇALE

8 best end of neck chops
salt & pepper
25 g. / 1 oz. lard
100 g. / 4 oz. small onions
1 crushed clove of garlic
100 g. / 4 oz. button mushrooms
425 g. / 15 oz. tin of tomatoes
1 tbsp. chopped parsley
1 tsp. cornflour

Season the chops and brown them on both sides in the hot fat. Put the chops in a casserole dish. Lightly brown the onions, garlic and mushrooms in the fat and add to the meat with the tomatoes and parsley.

Cover and cook in a preheated oven for 4 hours at 150° C. / 300° F. / gas 3. Just before serving blend the cornflour with a little of the cooking liquid and stir into the pot to thicken.

Slow cook pot: Low 8-10 hours. High 4-5 hours.

ROLLED LOIN OF LAMB

1 kg. / 2 lb. best end of lamb, boned and skinned
25 g. / 1 oz. butter
1 small onion, chopped
50 g. / 2 oz. breadcrumbs
25 g. / 1 oz. finely chopped walnuts
grated rind of ½ lemon
1 tbsp. chopped parsley
1 tbsp. chopped basil
salt & pepper
1 beaten egg

1 large sliced onion
225 ml. / 8 fl. oz. lamb stock
1 tsp. worcestershire sauce
1 tbsp. tomato puree
salt & pepper

Melt the butter and sauté the small onion, mix with the breadcrumbs, walnuts, lemon rind, herbs and seasoning, bind together with the egg. Spread this stuffing mixture over the lamb, roll up and tie with string.

Heat a little oil in a roasting dish on top of the stove and brown the joint all over. Put in a preheated oven and cook for 1 hour at 200 C./ 400 F./ gas 6.

Now make the sauce. Sauté the large onion until soft, then purée it; place in a saucepan with stock, worcestershire sauce and tomato purée, bring to the boil, stirring continuously and season.

Let the lamb stand for 5 minutes. Before untying, slice thickly and serve with the sauce.

SPICED PORK CHOPS

4 large pork chops
40 g. / 2 oz. brown sugar
½ tsp. ground cinnamon
¼ tsp. ground cloves
250 ml. / 8 fl. oz. tomato sauce
large tin of halved peaches
60 ml. / 2 fl. oz. white wine
salt & pepper

Lightly brown the chops in a frying pan, drain off fat; place in an ovendish. Mix together sugar, cinnamon, cloves, tomato sauce and 250 ml./ 8 fl. oz. of juice from the peaches, sprinkle the chops with salt and pepper, pour over the sauce mixture; place the drained peach halves on top, cover the dish and cook in a preheated oven 150° C. / 300° F. / gas 3 for 2½ hours.

Slow cook pot: This can be prepared very well in a cook pot, cook on Low for 5 hours or High for 2½ hours.

FRIED PORK SLICES

450 g. / 1 lb. thin pork steaks
1 egg, beaten
450 g. / 1 lb. sage & onion stuffing, as dry as possible
butter

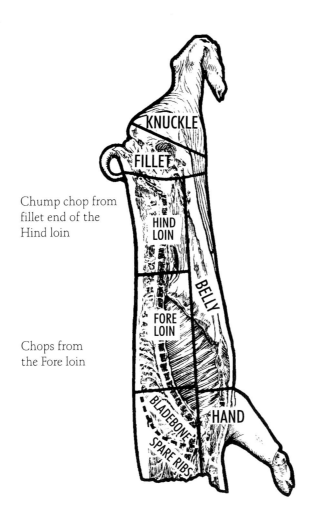

Chump chop from
fillet end of the
Hind loin

Chops from
the Fore loin

KNUCKLE

FILLET

HIND LOIN

BELLY

FORE LOIN

BLADEBONE

SPARE RIBS

HAND

ENGLISH CUTS OF PORK

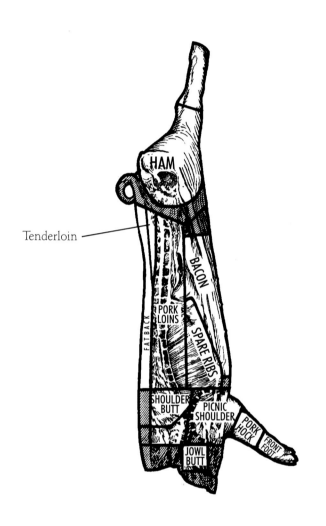

Tenderloin

HAM

BACON

PORK LOINS

FATBACK

SPARE RIBS

SHOULDER BUTT

PICNIC SHOULDER

PORK HOCK

FRONT FOOT

JOWL BUTT

AMERICAN CUTS OF PORK

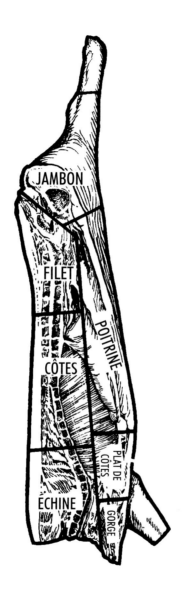

CONTINENTAL CUTS OF PORK

Beat the steaks flat and cut into portions, dip in the beaten egg and cover with the stuffing, quickly fry in the hot butter on both sides, then reduce the heat and continue to cook until brown and tender.

PORK CHOP NIÇOISE

4 large pork chops
seasoned flour
1 large chopped onion
1 large clove of garlic, crushed
450 g. / 1 lb. tomatoes, peeled, seeded and sliced
1 large green pepper, sliced
2 tbsp. tomato purée
1 tbsp. chopped basil
150 ml. / ¼ pt. white wine

Dust the chops in the seasoned flour, melt some butter in a deep frying pan and brown the chops all over, remove from the pan and keep warm. Put the onion and garlic in the pan and cook for 1 minute, add the tomatoes, pepper, tomato purée and the herbs; season well and add the wine. Place the chops on top, cover the pan and simmer for 45 minutes.

STUFFED ROAST PORK

1 kg. / 2 lb. loin of pork
60 g. / 2 oz. minced green pepper
60 g. / 2 oz. minced onion
1 clove of garlic, minced
60 ml. / 2 fl. oz. oil
450 g. / 1 lb. tomatoes, seeded and puréed
250 ml. / 8 fl. oz. hot water
1 tbsp. chilli powder
60 g. / 2 oz. brown sugar
½ tsp. salt
60 ml. / 2 fl. oz. water
140 g. / 5 oz. seedless raisins
80 g. / 3 oz. sliced olives
340 g. / 12 oz. cooked rice

Sauté the pepper, onion and garlic in the hot oil until soft, add the tomatoes and the hot water and bring to the boil. Mix the chilli powder, sugar, salt with the water and add this to the sauce with the raisins and olives, boil for 5 minutes. Take 60 ml. / 2 fl. oz. of this sauce and mix with the cooked rice.

With a very sharp knife loosen the pork from the bone to form a pocket, stuff this pocket with the rice mixture Put in an ovendish and cook, covered in a preheated oven for 1 hour at 175° C./ 350° F./ gas 4. Pour the rest of the sauce over the joint and continue to cook for 1-1½ hours basting frequently.

MARINATED ROAST PORK WITH APRICOT GLAZE

1½ kg. / 3 lb. pork rib joint
250 ml. / 8 fl. oz. red wine
1 tbsp. worcestershire sauce
1 tbsp. soy sauce
1 tbsp. Angostura Bitters
2 dashes Tabasco sauce
2 small onions, sliced
2 tbsp. tomato sauce
salt & pepper
250 ml. / 8 fl. oz. chicken stock
thick apricot jam

Marinate the pork for 12 hours in the red wine. Put the joint, fat side down in an ovendish, mix the marinating wine with the sauces and pour over the joint, place the onion slices on top and pour over the to-mato sauce, season with salt and pepper, cover and roast in a preheated oven for 1 hour at 160° C. / 320° F. / gas 3.

After 1 hour turn the joint and roast uncovered for another ½ hour. Then glaze the top with a thick coating of apricot jam, turn up the heat to maximum until the glaze bubbles. Serve with the pan juices, add a little more chicken stock if necessary during the cooking.

PORK STEAKS WITH ORANGE

4 pork steaks
2 tbsp. oil
2 thinly sliced onions
1 tbsp. butter
1 tsp. Dijon mustard
1 tbsp. brown sugar
grated rind of 2 oranges
2 tbsp. flour
300 ml. / ½ pt. chicken stock
150 ml. / ¼ pt. white wine
juice of 2 oranges
salt & pepper
100 g. / 4 oz. button mushrooms, sliced
1 large orange
chopped parsley

Heat the oil in a frying pan and saute the onions until soft, remove from pan. Mix the butter, mustard, sugar and orange rind into a paste, add to the pan with the pork steaks and saute until brown on both sides, remove from the pan.

Stir the flour into the pan juices and cook for 3-4 minutes, add the stock and the wine a little at a time, stirring over a medium heat until it thickens, bring to the boil and add the orange juice and seasoning.

Put the onions and steaks in an ovendish pour over the sauce, cover and cook in a preheated oven for 1½ hours at 180° C. / 350° F. / gas 4.

Add the mushrooms about 10 minutes before end of cooking.

Peel and pith the orange, divide into segments, add to the dish and sprinkle with parsley before serving.

PAN FRIED PORK STEAKS
This is a simple way of dressing up the normal pork or veal steaks.

Flatten the steaks with a rolling pin and dip each into seasoned beaten egg. Now toss them in dry sage and onion mix, the packet variety is ideal. Fry in hot lard on both sides for about 5 minutes, lower the heat and cook until brown and tender.

POULTRY

Today virtually all poultry is sold "oven ready", although at Christmas time some butchers still have fresh birds available but again these are usually plucked and drawn but may still have the head and feet in place. Make sure you have the gizzard, heart and liver. Cut off the head and feet. If you buy a frozen bird leave in a cool place to defrost thoroughly.

Make sure that the windpipe is removed, this is the almost clear plastic like tube running down the neck into the breast area. Wash the inside of the bird thoroughly, letting cold water run through from the tail end and out through the neck.

Pat the inside dry with kitchen paper and put in the preferred stuffing. Now the bird should be trussed, this is best done with a large darning needle and fine string, first sew up the tail end cavity; now stitch the wing pinions together leaving 2 long ends to the string, pass these ends crossing them over the back and tie them around the tail, fastening the legs at the same time.

Poultry can be cooked in any of the methods used for meat but it is usually roasted.

ROASTING TIMES etc.

TURKEY:
30 minutes per Kg. / 2 lb. for birds up to 7 Kg. / 14 lb.
20 minutes per Kg. / 2 lb. for larger birds.
Stuff with sausagemeat, chestnut or any forcemeat.
Usually served with giblets gravy, bread sauce, sausages and bacon rolls.

CHICKEN:
Roast for 1 hour.
Stuff with any forcemeat or sage and onion. Usually served with giblets gravy, bread sauce and sausages.

DUCK:
Roast for 1¼ hours. Stuff with sage and onion. Serve with gravy and apple sauce

GOOSE:
Roast for 1½ hours. Stuff with sage and onion. Serve with gravy and orange salad.

The breast of turkeys and chicken should be covered with some strips of fat bacon to prevent the meat from becoming too dry; geese and ducks do not require this precaution. Large birds requiring a long cooking time may need covering with greaseproof paper to prevent over browning.

All birds should be roasted on a trivet so that they do not sit in the juices, during roasting they should basted regularly with the juices; with geese there may be an excess of fat from the bird during cooking and this should be poured off.

To test whether cooking is complete take a fine skewer and pierce the upper thigh of the bird, the juices should run clear, any blood or discoloration means that cooking is not complete.

CHICKEN MARYLAND

4 large chicken joints
2 tbsp. flour
½ l. / ¾ pt. milk
4 tbsp. double cream
2 egg yolks
salt & pepper

Dip the chicken in milk and dust with seasoned flour, brown them all over in hot lard. Put them in a covered ovendish and cook in a preheated oven for ½ hour at 180° C. / 350° F. / gas 4. In the frying pan used to brown the chicken stir in the flour and cook for a few moments, pour in the milk a little at a time, stirring continuously until thick, add the cream, simmer gently for 15 minutes. Just before serving beat in the egg yolks and season.

Meanwhile make some corn fritters (page 25) and grill some streaky bacon rashers. Place the chicken joints, the fritters and bacon on a warm serving dish and pour the sauce into a jug.

Sometimes fried bananas are served as well, slice them down the middle, then half and fry gently in butter.

CHICKEN WITH LEMON AND ALMONDS

4 large chicken joints
1 large lemon
85 g. / 3 oz. butter
115 g. / 4 oz. sliced mushrooms
140 ml. / ¼ pt. cream
55 g. / 2 oz. blanched, split almonds
salt & pepper

Squeeze ½ lemon over the chicken, slowly fry the joints in butter on both sides until tender, remove from the pan and keep warm.

Lightly fry the mushrooms, then pour on the cream and slowly bring to the boil, add the bulk of the almonds and season.

Pour the sauce over the chicken and sprinkle on the rest of the almonds.

CREAM OF CHICKEN PIE

225 g. / 8 oz. shortcrust pastry
450 g. / 1 lb. diced cooked chicken
125 ml. / 4 fl. oz. chicken stock
60 g. / 2 oz. chopped green pepper
pinch of rosemary
salt & pepper
300 ml. / 10 oz. can of cream of chicken soup
2 beaten eggs
112 g. / 4 oz. sliced mushrooms
45 g. / 1½ oz. breadcrumbs
2 tbsp. butter

Line a deep 23 cm / 9 in. pie dish with the pastry and bake in a preheated oven for 5 minutes at 230° C. / 450° F. / gas 8.

Mix together the chicken, stock, green pepper, rosemary, soup, eggs and season, place in the pastry lined pie dish and cook in a preheated oven for 30 minutes at 175° C. / 350° F. / gas 4. Sauté the mushrooms and breadcrumbs in butter and sprinkle over the top 5 minutes before baking is complete.

Turkey can be used instead of chicken and celery instead of green pepper.

CHICKEN BREASTS CORDON BLEU

2 whole chicken breasts
2 slices swiss cheese
2 thin slices boiled ham
30 g. / 1 oz. butter
200 g. / 8 oz. can condensed mushroom soup
30 ml. / 1 fl. oz. milk
15 ml. / ½ fl. oz. sherry
salt & pepper

Skin and bone the chicken, split in half and flatten with mallet; cut the slices of cheese and ham in half. Put a slice of ham and cheese on each half breast and secure with toothpicks.

Melt the butter in a frying pan and brown the chicken side only, place in an oven dish, mix together the remaining ingredients, pour over the chicken, cover and cook for 3 hours at 150° C. / 200° F. / gas 3.

Slow cook pot: High for 3 hours.

CHICKEN PAPRIKA

1½ kg. / 4 lb. chicken in pieces
225 g. / 8 oz. can of tomatoes
1 chopped green pepper
1 sliced small onion
10 g. / ¾ oz. paprika
1 crushed clove garlic
salt & pepper
¼ tsp. oregano
30 g. / 1 oz. flour
200 ml. / 6 fl. oz. sour cream
300 ml. / ½ pt. water

Put all the ingredients into a casserole and bring to the boil, simmer gently for 3 to 4 hours until chicken is tender.

Remove the chicken pieces, skim off the fat from the liquid. Blend the flour with 75 ml. / 2 fl. oz. of cooled liquid, stir into the liquid in the pot until thickened, then blend in the cream, return the chicken pieces and heat through but do not boil. Serve with rice or noodles.

Slow cook pot: Low for 8 hours, then High when blending in the flour and cream.

CHICKEN CHASSEUR

1 kg. / 2½ lbs. chicken pieces
salt & pepper
flour
2 chopped shallots
12 chopped mushrooms
100 ml. / 4 fl. oz. dry white wine
2 chopped tomatoes
1 tsp. chopped parsley
¼ tsp. tarragon

Season the chicken, roll in flour and brown in hot oil in frying pan, place in an oven dish.

Sauté the shallots and mushrooms in the frying pan for a few minutes then add the remaining ingredients, when well blended pour over the chicken and cook for 4 hours at 150° C. / 300° F. / gas 3

Slow cook pot: Low for 6 hours.

CHICKEN MARENGO

1 kg. / 2½ lbs. chicken pieces
6 small onions
250 g. / ½ lb. mushrooms
2 chopped shallots
1 crushed clove garlic
salt & pepper
1 tsp. thyme
2 sprigs parsley
1 bay leaf
50 g. / 2 oz. stuffed olives, sliced
225 g. / 8 oz. can tomatoes
50 ml. / 2 fl. oz. dry white wine

Put onions in the bottom of an oven dish and add the chicken and sliced mushrooms, mix all the remaining ingredients and add to the pot, cook for 3 hours at 150 C. / 300 F. / gas 3.

Slow cook pot: Low 7 hours or High 3 hours.

CHICKEN CACCIATORE

1 kg. / 2½ lbs. chicken pieces
2 sliced medium onions
2 crushed cloves garlic
¾ kg. / 1½ lbs. tomatoes
1 chopped green pepper
salt & pepper
1 tsp. oregano
½ tsp. basil
½ tsp. celery salt
¼ tsp. cayenne
1 crumbled bay leaf
125 ml. / 4 fl. oz. dry red wine

Brown the chicken in hot oil in a frying pan, place in an oven dish, cover with the onion and add all the remaining ingredients. Cook for 3 hours at 150° C. / 300° F. / gas 3.
Slow cook pot: Low for 7 hours or High for 3 hours.

CHICKEN TETRAZZINI

1 kg. / 2½ lb. chicken
1 medium sliced onion
1 small chopped green pepper
115 g. / 4 oz. chopped mushrooms
1½ tbsp. minced pimiento
1 tbsp. butter
1 tbsp. flour
salt & pepper
200 ml. / 6 fl. oz. milk
30 ml. / 1 fl. oz. sherry
300 g./ 10 oz. box of spaghetti
30 g. / 1 oz. grated parmesan cheese

Boil the chicken until meat comes off the bones, save the stock. When cool, cube the meat. Sauté in butter the onion, pepper and mushrooms, mix with the chicken and pimiento. Now blend the flour in the heated butter and add the milk a little at a time stirring continuosly until medium thick and add the sherry. Mix in the chicken and warm through.

Cook the spaghetti in the chicken stock adding water if necessary, when cooked, drain and add to the chicken mixture and stir in the grated cheese, put in a greased oven dish, sprinkle generously with some more grated parmesan and bake in a pre-heated oven for 25 minutes at 190° C. / 375° F. / gas 5.

DUCK A L'ORANGE

1½ kg. / 3 lb. duckling
25 g. / 1 oz. flour
salt & pepper
25 g. / 1 oz. butter
1 chopped small onion
50 g. / 2 oz. sliced mushrooms
1 large orange
250 ml. / ½ pt. fresh orange juice
2 tsp. flour
watercress, optional

Cut the duck into 4 portions and coat with seasoned flour, fry the duck in butter until lightly brown then place in a casserole dish. Lightly fry the onions and mushrooms and add to the dish with the grated rind of the orange and the orange juice. Cover and cook in a preheated oven for 4 hours at 150° C. / 300° F. / gas 3, ½ hours before serving stir in the blended flour and baste the duck well.

To serve slice the orange and place on the duck portions, garnish with watercress.

Slow cook pot: Low 8-10 hours, High 4-5 hours.

ROAST DUCK WITH RICE STUFFING

1½ kg. / 3 lb. duck
1 quartered orange
2 tbsp. lemon juice
salt & pepper
60 ml. / 1 fl. oz. sherry

Stuff the duck with the orange, put breast side up on a rack in a shallow roasting pan, sprinkle with lemon juice and salt, roast for 1½ hours at 165° C. / 325° F. / gas 3. Pour off the fat, add the sherry to the pan and continue cooking for another 1 hour, basting regularly.

Skim the fat from the pan drippings and prepare a gravy.

Rice stuffing

225 g. / 8 oz. brown or wild rice
60 g. / 2 oz. butter
60 g. / 2 oz. chopped onion
225 g. / 8 oz. sliced mushrooms
750 ml. / 24 fl. oz. chicken or mushroom stock
pinch of basil
salt & pepper
50 g. / 2 oz. breadcrumbs

Wash and drain the rice, slowly sauté rice, onion and mushrooms in the butter, when rice begins to turn yellow stir in the rest of the ingredients, cover and simmer until all the moisture is absorbed, about 1¼ hours.

Carve the duck discarding the orange pieces, arrange on a bed of the rice stuffing and pour over the gravy.

FRUITY DUCK

2 kg. / 4 lb. duck
salt
1 medium chopped onion
1 large chopped cooking apple
60 g. / 2 oz. chopped celery
2 tbsp. chopped parsley
120 ml. / 4 fl. oz. apple juice
30 g. / 2 oz. butter
30 ml. / 1 fl. oz. brandy

Clean and dry the duck, sprinkle the inside with salt and stuff with a mixture of onion, apple, celery and parsley. Place on a rack in a shallow roasting dish and roast for 1 hour at 165° C. / 325° F. / gas 3; pour off the fat and add the remaining ingredients to the pan, continue roasting and basting until duck is tender, about 1½ hours.

Remove the duck from the pan and keep warm. Skim any fat from the pan drippings, add more apple juice to make 180 ml. / 6 fl. oz., stir in a tbsp. of flour, cook and stir until thickened and smooth.

DUCK WITH MANDARINS

2 kg. / 4 lb. duck
30 ml. / 1 fl. oz. lemon juice
2 tbsp. flour
1 tsp. ground ginger
salt
crushed clove of garlic
30 ml. /1 fl. oz. oil
60 g. / 2 oz. chopped celery
60 ml./ 2 fl. oz. sherry
1 tsp. soya sauce
½ tsp. curry powder
240 ml . / 8 fl. oz. chicken stock
60 g. / 1 oz. sliced green onion
1 tbsp. butter
1 tbsp. flour
250 g. / 10 oz. tin drained mandarin oranges

Skin the duck and remove any heavy fat, brush with lemon juice and sprinkle with the flour, ginger, salt and garlic and cut into pieces. Lightly brown the duck in hot oil and place in a casserole. Pour out all the fat from the saute pan and put in the celery, sherry, soy sauce, curry powder, stock and onion, heat and stir until well mixed, pour over the duck, cover and cook in a preheated oven for 1 hour at 175° C. / 350° F. / gas 4.

Drain the juices into a pan, skim off the fat and bring to the boil, blend in a smooth paste of the flour and butter and cook until thickened, stir in the mandarins. Pour the sauce over the duck and continue cooking until tender, about ½ hour.

Serve on a bed of rice.

BASIC STOCKS, SAUCES STUFFINGS, ETC.

Many meals can be enhanced, brought up to good restaurant standard, by the addition of a sauce. Many of the sauces in this section, especially the brown variety keep well when frozen.

WHITE STOCK or CHICKEN STOCK

450 g. / 1 lb. veal bones or chicken carcass
500 ml. / 1 pt. water
1 small onion, sliced
1 small carrot, sliced
1 small stalk celery, chopped
little thyme & parsley
1 bay leaf
1 clove
little mace
salt & pepper

Place the bones in a pan with the water, leave to stand for about an hour, bring to the boil and add the other ingredients, simmer gently for 3 hours. Strain through a fine sieve, cool and remove any fat. If using a recipe requiring cooked chicken meat, put the complete bird in the pan and proceed as above.

Remove the bird after 45 minutes, remove the skin and the bones and return these to the pan and continue as above.

FISH STOCK

As for White Stock but using a cheap white fish complete with bones and trimmings.

BROWN STOCK

As for White Stock but using a cheap cut of beef, like shin with the bones, it helps if the bones are crushed.

BECHAMEL SAUCE

For creamed poultry, fish, seafood, eggs, vegetables and as a base for other sauces.

350 ml. / 12 fl. oz. milk
½ tbsp. grated onion
sprig of parsley
salt & pepper
few grains of nutmeg
1 tbsp. butter
2 tbsp. flour

Melt butter in a saucepan, remove from the heat, stir in the flour and salt until mixture is smooth, cook over a gentle heat until it bubbles and begins to turn golden brown, stir continuosly.

Meanwhile scald the milk with the onion, strain and add to the pan stirring briskly with a wire whisk until blended and smooth; bring to the boil then reduce the heat and cook slowly, stirring frequently until reduced to about 2/3 rds. of original quantity.

VELOUTE SAUCE

For creamed poultry, eggs and as a base for other sauces.

350 ml. / 12 fl. oz. White Stock
1 tbsp. butter
2 tbsp. flour
salt & pepper
125 g. / 2 oz. mushrooms, chopped

Melt the butter in a pan, remove from the heat and stir in the flour until mixture is smooth; cook over a low heat until it starts to turn golden brown, remove from the heat and add the boiling stock stirring briskly until blended and smooth.

Add the seasonings and mushrooms, bring to the boil, then reduce heat and cook slowly, stirring frequently until reduced to about 2/3 rds. original quantity, about 30 minutes; strain through a fine sieve.

FISH VELOUTE SAUCE
For poached fish
As Veloute Sauce but using Fish Stock

BROWN SAUCE

1 tbsp. butter, for roux
2 tbsp. flour for roux
1 tbsp . butter
½ chopped carrot
1 small stalk celery chopped
1 medium onion chopped
425 ml. / ¾ pt. Brown Stock
3 peppercorns
bouquet garni of parsley, thyme & bay leaf
small clove garlic
1 tomato chopped or little tomato purée

Make a brown roux by melting the butter in a pan, remove from the heat and blend in the flour until smooth, return to the heat and cook gently until rich brown colour.

Melt butter in saucepan and add chopped vegetables cover and cook gently for 3-4 minutes, uncover and continue to cook until everything is golden brown, stir in the brown roux and blend thoroughly.

Add stock, peppercorns, bouquet garni and garlic, cook and stir until boiling, reduce heat and simmer for 1 hour, skim off any fat or scum. Strain through a fine sieve, add tomato and simmer for another hour, strain and cool.

ESPAGNOLE SAUCE

250 ml. / 8 fl. oz. Brown Sauce
1 tbsp. meat extract
2 tbsp. dry Sherry

Cook the sauce on low heat until reduced by 1/3 rd, about 25 minutes, add meat extract and simmer for 15 minutes add sherry and simmer for 5 minutes.

THIN WHITE SAUCE
For cream soups or creamed vegetables

1 tbsp. butter
I tbsp. flour
½ tsp. salt
pinch of pepper
pinch of paprika
225 ml. / 8 fl. oz. milk

Melt the butter in a pan, remove from the heat and blend in the flour, cook over low heat for about 1 minute. **Do NOT** brown; remove from the heat, add seasonings and gradually blend in the milk until mixture is smooth. Bring to the boil over medium heat and cook for 5 minutes stirring continuosly.

MEDIUM WHITE SAUCE
For creamed fish, eggs & escallops

As for Thin White Sauce but using 2 tbsp. of both flour and butter.

THICK WHITE SAUCE
For soufflés

As for Thin White Sauce but using 3 tbsp. of both flour and butter.

VERY THICK WHITE SAUCE
For croquettes

As for Thin White Sauce but using 4 tbsp. of both flour and butter.

A LA KING SAUCE
For chicken, turkey and hard cooked eggs

1 tbsp. butter
115 g. / 4 oz. sliced mushrooms
350 ml. / 12 fl. oz. Hot Bechamel or Medium White Sauce
1 pimiento cut in narrow strips

2 egg yolks lightly beaten
125 ml. / 4 fl. oz. medium cream
1 tbsp. dry Sherry

Melt butter in a pan, add mushrooms and cook for 5 minutes, do not brown, stir in the hot sauce and add pimiento.

Mix the egg yolks and the cream and slowly stir in half of the hot sauce then stir this egg mix into the rest of the sauce; cook and stir until nearly boiling then add the Sherry

BERCY SAUCE
For baked or grilled fish

1 tbsp. butter
1 tbsp. finely chopped shallots
60 ml. / 2 fl. oz. white wine
250 ml. / 8 fl. oz. hot Fish Veloute Sauce
1 tsp. butter
1 tsp. lemon juice
pinch cayenne pepper
1 tsp. chopped parsley

Melt the butter in a pan, add the shallots and cook for a few mins. Do NOT brown, add the wine and reduce by half. Then add the hot Fish Veloute Sauce and blend well, add the butter, lemon juice and pepper, cook slowly for 5 minutes. Add the parsley just before serving.

WHITE BORDELAISE or LIGHT BORDELAISE SAUCE
For fish or veal

3 shallots finely chopped
250 ml. / 8 fl. oz. white wine
250 ml. / 8 fl. oz. hot Velouté Sauce
1 tsp. chopped tarragon
1 tsp. butter

Cook shallots in wine until wine is almost gone, add the Veloute Sauce and simmer for 15 minutes, strain through a fine sieve, add tarragon and finally the butter.

MORNAY SAUCE
For fish, poultry and eggs

1 egg yolk
1 tbsp. thick cream
250 ml. / 8 fl. oz. hot Bechamel Sauce
½ tbsp. grated parmesan cheese
½ tbsp. grated gruyere cheese
½ tbsp. whipped cream

Stir egg yolk and cream together, slowly add about 1/3rd. the hot Bechamel Sauce, return this mixture to the rest of the sauce. Cook and stir over low heat until nearly boiling, remove from the heat and stir in the cheese until it melts and blends then fold in the whipped cream.

BORDELAISE SAUCE
For grilled steaks & chops

1 tbsp. finely chopped shallots
60 ml. / 2 fl. oz. red wine
250 ml / 8 fl. oz. hot Espagnole Sauce
2 tbsp, beef marrow or 1 tbsp. meat extract
60 ml. / 2 fl. oz. water
little chopped parsley

Cook shallots in wine until reduced by 1/3rd., add the hot Espagnole Sauce and simmer for 15 minutes.
Meantime poach the beef marrow in the water for 3 minutes or reduce the meat extract in the water, and add this liquid to the sauce. Add the parsley just before serving.

CHASSEUR SAUCE
For poultry, beef, lamb & game

225 g. / ½ lb. sliced mushrooms
2 tbsp. butter
salt & pepper
½ tbsp. finely chopped shallots
60 ml. /2 fl. oz. white wine

125 ml. / 4 fl. oz. hot Brown Sauce
1 tbsp. tomato purée
little chopped parsley & tarragon

Melt the butter in a saucepan, add the mushrooms, salt & pepper and cook gently until golden brown. Add shallots and wine and cook until reduced by half. Add the hot Brown Sauce and tomato purée, bring to the boil, remove from the heat and stir in the herbs.

CHATEAU SAUCE
For veal, lamb & chicken

1 tbsp. finely chopped shallots
60 ml. / 2 fl. oz. white wine
350 ml. / 12 fl. oz. hot Espagnole Sauce
90 g. / 3 oz. butter
little chopped parsley

Cook shallots in wine until liquid almost gone, pour in hot Espagnole Sauce, blend and cook slowly for 10 minutes. Remove from the heat and blend in the butter whisking as it melts, add the parsley.

ROBERT SAUCE
For roast pork or chops

1 tbsp. butter
1 small finely chopped onion
129 ml. / 4 fl. oz. white wine
1 tbsp. wine vinegar
250 ml / 8 fl. oz. hot Espagnole Sauce
1 tsp. dry mustard
¼ tsp. sugar
little chopped parsley

Cook onion in the butter until soft and golden, add wine and vinegar and cook until reduced by a third. Stir in the hot Espagnole Sauce and simmer for 20 minutes. Add mustard, sugar and parsley. **Do NOT** allow to boil again.

BEARNAISE SAUCE
For beef & fish

2 tbsp. finely chopped shallots
¼ tsp. dried tarragon
¼ tsp. dried chervil
salt
little cayenne pepper
110 ml. / 4 fl. oz. tarragon or wine vinegar
110 ml. / 4 fl. oz. white wine
2 egg yolks
1 tsp. lemon juice
¼ tsp. dried tarragon
¼ tsp. dried chervil

Cook shallots and seasonings in wine vinegar and wine until reduced by half, strain and cool. Add the egg yolks and put in the top of a double saucepan with hot **NOT** boiling water in the bottom, whisk until sauce starts to thicken, remove from the heat and beat in the lemon juice, then stir in the additional herbs.

RAISIN SAUCE
For baked or boiled ham and tongue

1 tbsp. butter
1 tbsp. flour
225 ml. / 8 fl. oz. water
40 g. / 1 oz. light brown sugar
70 g. / 2½ oz. seedless raisins
1 tbsp. lemon juice
60 ml. / 2 fl. oz. orange juice
little grated orange peel

Melt the butter in a saucepan, stir in the flour and cook for 1 minute; remove from the heat and add the water gradually, stirring all the time until smooth.
Bring to the boil stirring continuosly and cook until sauce has started to thicken, stir in the sugar and raisins; cover the pan and leave over very low heat for 10 minutes. Just before serving add lemon juice and grated peel.

CUMBERLAND SAUCE
For duck, ham, tongue & game

2 tbsp. finely slivered orange peel
80 ml. / 3 fl. oz. water
250 g. / 10 oz. red currant jelly
60 ml. / 2 fl. oz. port wine
60 ml. / 2 fl. oz. orange juice
1 tsp. cornstarch
1 tsp. dry mustard
¼ tsp. ground ginger
little cayenne pepper
1 tsp. lemon juice

Boil orange peel rapidly in the water, drain and reserve. Melt the jelly in a pan over a low heat, add the wine and orange juice. Mix cornstarch, mustard and spices together add the lemon juice to make a smooth paste, then stir briskly into the pan, bring to the boil and simmer for about 5 minutes, sauce should be clear and slightly thickened. Add the orange peel and use hot or cold.

BASIC TOMATO SAUCE
This is really ideal if you have a large quantity of home grown tomatoes, firm with a good flavour, not much use with the salad variety found in the supermarket.

1 kg. / 2 lb. tomatoes, skinned & chopped
1 large onion, chopped
3 chopped cloves garlic
125 g. / 4 oz. chopped streaky bacon
30 g. / 1 oz. butter
1 diced large carrot
150 ml. / 5 fl. oz. dry white wine
salt, pepper & sugar
dried oregano & chopped fresh basil

Soften the garlic, onion and bacon in the fat, add carrot, tomatoes and wine, raise the heat and cook for 15 minutes. Add the seasoning and cook for a further 5 minutes to obtain a stiff puree moist not watery. This freezes well and can be used in many other dishes.

GENERAL MARINADE
For all meats & poultry

250 ml. / 8 fl. oz. red wine for meat, white for poultry
2 tbsp. tarragon vinegar
4 tbsp. olive oil
1 medium onion finely sliced
1 finely chopped shallot
1 small carrot finely sliced
1 stalk celery chopped
1 crushed glove garlic
pinch of dried thyme
2 sprigs parsley
small bay leaf
5 peppercorns or ¼ tsp. ground pepper
1 clove

Mix all the ingredients together and use to marinate.

BOLOGNESE SAUCE
For spaghetti, lasagne etc.

1 tbsp. olive oil
2 tbsp. butter
115 g. / 4 oz. lean ham chopped
1 medium onion chopped
1 small carrot chopped
1 stalk celery chopped
225 g. / 8 oz. minced beef
115 g. / 4 oz. chicken livers chopped
2 tbsp. tomato puree
125 ml. / 4 fl. oz. white wine
250 ml. / 8 fl. oz. chicken stock
little nutmeg
salt & pepper
250 ml. / 8 fl. oz. cream

Heat oil and butter in a saucepan, add the ham, onion carrot and celery and cook for 10 minutes until vegetables begin to brown; add the minced beef, cook and stir until mixture is evenly brown throughout.

Stir in the chicken livers and cook for another 5 minutes. Then stir in tomato puree, wine, stock and nutmeg, reduce heat, cover the pan and simmer for 40 minutes, check seasonings and add the cream when cooking is complete.

RICH GIBLET GRAVY
for roast poultry

2 tbsp. olive oil
All the giblets including liver finely chopped
2 tbsp. flour
2 tbsp. tomato puree
850 ml. / 30 fl. oz. chicken stock
150 ml. / 5 fl. oz. sherry
salt & pepper
bouquet garni

Heat oil in heavy pan until smoking hot and brown the giblets, smear them with the tomato puree and brown, sprinkle in the flour and stir well until everything is well browned.

Remove the giblets, lower the heat and pour in the sherry, stir well until it collects all the bits in the pan and boils, return the giblets, pour in the stock, add the bouquet garni and bring to the boil; simmer for 45 minutes when gravy should look clear, check the seasonings and strain.

NOTE: The quantities given are for a medium sized turkey, adjust for a chicken

GARLIC BUTTER

250 g. / 8 oz. unsalted butter
50 g. / 1½ oz. chopped parsley
30 g. / 1 oz. chopped shallot
4 large cloves crushed garlic
1 tsp. black pepper
2 tsp. salt

Cream the butter and then mix in the other ingredients.

BERCY BUTTER
For grilled steaks & chops

125 ml. / 4 fl. oz. white wine
2 tbsp. finely chopped shallots
60 g. / 2 oz. butter
1 tbsp. chopped parsley
salt & pepper

Cook shallots in wine until reduced by half, leave to cool. Cream the butter add the parsley then stir into the cooled wine mix; check seasoning.

MAÎTRE D' HÔTEL BUTTER
For grilled meats & fish

120 g. / 4 oz. butter
1 tsp. chopped parsley
1 tbsp. lemon juice
salt & pepper

Cream the butter and blend in the other ingredients.

GREEK RICE STUFFING
This is one of a variety of Eastern Mediterranean stuffings used for various vegetable.

250 g. / ½ lb. minced beef
125 g. / 4 oz. long grain rice
1 chopped medium onion
30 ml. / 2 tbsp. tomato concentrate
2 tsp. salt
1 tsp. pepper
1 tbsp. chopped parsley
1 tsp. chopped mint
1 tsp. dill weed
2 tbsp. oil
¼ tsp. ground cinnamon

Mix everything together to make a totally infused mixture; use to stuff various vegetables as directed in the particular recipe.

SAGE & ONION STUFFING

2 large onions
2 tbsp. butter
115 g. / 4 oz. breadcrumbs
3 tbsp. dried sage
salt & pepper

Put the onions in cold water and boil for 5 minutes, strain off the water and add fresh boiling water and cook until tender.

Drain well and chop very finely, then add the other ingredients and mix well.

SAUSAGE STUFFING

1 large chopped onion
450 g. / 1 lb. pork sausage meat
2 tbsp. dripping or margarine
1 tsp. chopped parsley
½ tsp. mixed herbs
60 g. / 2 oz. breadcrumbs
salt & pepper

Mix onion and sausage meat and saute in the melted fat for a few minutes then mix in the other ingredients.

BREAD SAUCE
To accompany roast poultry

2 tbsp. butter
60 g. / 2 oz. chopped onion
1 crushed clove garlic
60 g. / 2 oz. breadcrumbs
250 ml. / 8 fl. oz. rich milk
150 ml. / 5 fl. oz. double cream
¼ tsp. ground mace
pinch of salt
Using a double saucepan melt the butter and soften the onion

without colouring; add the garlic, breadcrumbs, milk, mace and salt; cover and cook for 30 minutes. Blend to a fine purée, stir in the cream and reheat.

FRENCH SALAD DRESSING

1 tsp. salt
½ tsp. pepper
1 tsp. dry mustard
pinch of sugar
4 tbsp. vinegar
4 tbsp. olive oil

Mix all the ingredients, except the oil, together then beat in the oil. This mixture will separate and must be beaten or shaken before use.

PASTRY

Cool working conditions and a hot oven are essential for good pastry, it should be handled as little as possible and the fat rubbed in with the tips of the fingers. Flaky and puff pastry mixes are better by being left to cool between rollings, and by being left in a cool place for several hours before baking.

Always measure the ingredients carefully and sieve the dry ingredients; careful mixing is essential, too much liquid will give a sticky, unmanageable dough. The pastry should be rolled as little as possible and lightly, avoid stretching as it will shrink back during baking.

SHORTCRUST PASTRY
For pies, sausage rolls etc.

115 g. / 4 oz. flour
Pinch of salt
60 g. / 2 oz. fat
COLD water to mix

Sieve the dry ingredients into a mixing bowl, rub in the fat using the finger tips, mix with cold water using a knife, add only just enough water to bind together, finish the mixing with the fingers. Roll out as required on a floured board but lightly.

PUFF PASTRY

May be used for sweet and savoury dishes but being the richest and lightest of pastries is usually only used on special occasions. It must be worked very lightly, allow to cool between rollings, better if made the day before use and left to become cold and firm before cutting out. It must be cooked in a hot oven 475° F. / 240° C. / gas 9.

225 g. / 8 oz. flour
225 g. / 8 oz. unsalted butter
Pinch of salt
Squeeze of lemon juice
COLD water to mix

Sieve the flour and salt and rub in about 60 g. / 2 oz. of fat, mix with the lemon juice and water into a dough and knead until smooth.

Roll the pastry into a square, form the rest of the fat into an oblong the length of the square and half as wide, place the fat on one half of the pastry and fold the rest over sealing the edges.

Turn the pastry so that fold is on the right, roll into a strip, fold into three, seal the edges lightly and leave to cool. Turn the pastry so that fold is on the right and repeat the rolling, folding and cooling until it has been done a total of 6 times.

ECCLES CAKES

Puff pastry using 115 g. / 4 oz. flour etc.
30 g. / 1 oz. margarine
115 g. / 4 oz. currants
30 g. / 1 oz. mixed peel
Grated nutmeg
Spice
30 g. / 1 oz. sugar
Egg white and sugar to glaze

Roll out the pastry and cut into circles using a large cutter or saucer. Melt the fat and add the fruit peel, spices to taste and the sugar. Put a spoonful of this mixture on each piece of pastry, damp the edges and draw together to enclose the filling.

Slit across the surface of the pastry with a knife, then roll over each cake lightly so that the filling shows through, glaze with egg white and a little sugar, bake in a hot oven for 15-20 minutes 450° F / 220° C / gas 7.

VANILLA SLICES

Puff pastry using 175 g. / 6 oz. flour
Cream or thick custard
Vanilla essence
Raspberry or strawberry jam
White glace icing

Roll the pastry 6 cm / ¼ in. thick into a strip 100 cm / 4 in. wide, then cut into oblong pieces about 4 cm / 1½ in. wide and bake in a hot oven for 10 minutes 475° F. / 230° C. / gas 9. Leave until quite cold. Mix together the cream and the vanilla essence and make a sandwich of two of the pastry slices with jam and the cream, top the sandwich with a little glace icing. Serve as a cold dessert or for tea.

FLAKY PASTRY

This is similar to puff pastry but not as rich, i.e. not as much fat and is a little more tedious to make; if a recipe calls for flaky pastry it is generally easier to use puff or rough puff in its place.

ROUGH PUFF PASTRY

This may be used for any dish for which puff or flaky is called for. The fat can be a mixture of margarine and white fat. Coolness is vital.

225 g. / 8 oz. flour
Pinch of salt
145 g. / 5 oz. fat
Squeeze of lemon juice
COLD water to mix

Sieve the flour and the salt and add the fat cut into pieces; mix with the lemon juice and sufficient cold water to make a stiff dough.

Roll out on a lightly floured board into a long strip, keep the edges straight. Fold the bottom third up and then fold the top third down over it. Turn the pastry so that the folded edge is on the right; repeat the rolling and folding 4 times leave to get really cold and use for sausage rolls etc.

FLAN PASTRY

This is a richer, sweetened pastry of the shortcrust type, suitable for flans, cold desserts and tea pastries.

115 g. / 4 oz. flour
Pinch of salt
60 g. / 2 oz. fat
1 tsp. sugar
1 egg yolk
COLD water to mix

Sieve the flour and salt and rub in the fat; add the sugar and mix with the egg yolk and enough cold water to make a stiff dough; knead slightly until smooth.

MAKING A FLAN CASE

Place a flan ring on greaseproof paper on a baking sheet, roll out the pastry and line the flan case without stretching it, trim the top edge and put in a sheet of greaseproof paper and fill it with baking beans. Bake in a hot oven, 425° F. / 210° C. / gas 8 for 10 minutes, remove the greaseproof paper and the baking beans and continue to bake for another 5 minutes. A sandwich tin can be used in place of a flan ring.

FRUIT FLANS

The baked flan case can be filled with fresh, tinned or lightly stewed fruit, drained free of juice. Raspberries and strawberries are best fresh and uncooked, plums and apricots etc. are better lightly stewed; apples and pears should be quickly covered with lemon juice when peeled before stewing to keep their colour.

Make a jelly glaze by dissolving 1 tsp. of gelatine in 150 ml. / ¼ pt. of the sweetened fruit juice; when it begins to set pour over the fruit.

If using a propriety brand of gelatine use the instructions on the packet.

SUET CRUST PASTRY

This is used for both sweet and savoury dishes. It can also be boiled or steamed unlike other pastries. It is much easier to use one of the prepared suets sold in packets.

225 g. / 8 oz. flour
½ tsp. salt
115 g. / 4 oz. suet
COLD water to mix

Sieve the flour and salt, add the suet then mix with the cold water to a soft NOT sticky dough. Knead lightly, roll out on a lightly floured board as required.

SUET DUMPLINGS

Use the basic recipe but add extra salt, herbs maybe added as well. Form into small balls and add to the soup or stew 20 minutes before serving.

STEAK AND KIDNEY PUDDING

Suet pastry using 225 g. / 8 oz. flour
450 g. / 1 lb. stewing steak cut into cubes
seasoned flour
115 g. / 4 oz. kidney, skinned, cored and cubed
Little chopped onion
60 g. / 2 oz. chopped mushrooms (optional)
3 tbsp. beef stock

Grease a 150 cm / 6 in. pudding basin and line it with ¾ of the pastry. Roll the steak and the kidney in seasoned flour and fill the basin with the meat, onion, mushrooms and the stock; put on a pastry top sealing the edges. Cover with greased paper or a cloth and steam for at least 3 hours.

When cooked remove the paper or cloth and have a small amount of hot stock ready to add to the pudding when opened.

FRUIT PUDDING

Make as for Steak and kidney but put 450-675 g. / 1-1½ lb. prepared fruit, 115 g. / 4 oz. sugar and a little water in the lined basin. When cooked turn out onto a warm dish and serve with custard.

MINCEMEAT

450 g. / 1 lb. mixed fruit
60 g. / 2 oz. candied peel
60 g. / 2 oz. shelled nuts
2 small apples
115 g. /4 oz. suet
180 g. / 6 oz. brown sugar
½ tsp. mixed spice
½ tsp. grated nutmeg
2 tsp. lemon juice
Brandy

Mince coarsely the fruit, peel, nuts and apples; add the suet, sugar, spices and lemon juice and leave overnight.

Add brandy to taste and to give a good consistency, stir very thoroughly and pack into dry jars. This mixture should keep for many months.

CHRISTMAS PUDDING

180 g. / 6 oz. flour
½ tsp. mixed spice
¼ tsp. grated nutmeg
60 g. / 2 oz. breadcrumbs
115 g. / 4 oz. suet
675 g. / 1½ lb. mixed dried fruit
grated rind of 1 orange
1 finely chopped apple
90 g. / 3 oz. sugar
3 eggs, beaten
few drops of almond essence
few drops of vanilla essence
1 tsp. lemon juice
milk and brandy to mix; the more brandy the better for keeping

Sieve the flour and spices into a large mixing bowl, add the rest of the dry ingredients and mix thoroughly, mix in the eggs and essences; then add the milk and brandy to give a stiff dropping consistency.

Fill one or more (depending on size) greased pudding basins ¾ full, cover with greased paper and a pudding cloth and steam for 6 hrs.

Leave pudding to dry, remove the pudding cloth but leave the greased paper covering, put on a clean pudding cloth and store in a cool, dry place until needed then steam for about 1½ hrs., turn out and serve with Brandy Butter.

This pudding will keep for many months.

BATTERS

The mixture of eggs, milk and flour, called a batter is used for a number of puddings, pancakes and fritters.

These batters must be well beaten to entrap air which expands during the cooking.

BASIC RECIPE

115 g. / 4 oz. flour
¼ tsp. salt
1 egg
300 ml. / ½ pt. milk

Sieve the flour and salt into a mixing bowl, make a well in the middle and drop in the egg, add half the milk gradually and mix until smooth. Now beat the mixture with the back of a wooden spoon for about 10 minutes. The surface should now be covered with bubbles, now stir in the rest of the milk.

The beating can be done in a mixing machine.

PANCAKES

Batter made with 300 ml. / ½ pt. milk
Lard
Lemon
Sugar

Melt a lump of lard in a smooth frying pan, pour off any excess, when fat is smoking hot pour in just enough batter to just cover the pan, cook gently for 1 or 2 minutes, turn it over and cook the other side.

When you are well practised you will be able to do this by tossing it up. Place on a hot plate and sprinkle with sugar and lemon juice.

COATING BATTER

Make as the basic recipe but using only half the quantity of milk. For an economic batter for dishes like fish ,the egg may be omitted.

RICH COATING BATTER

Make as Coating Batter above but just before using fold in two stiffly beaten egg whites.

This mixture can be used for fruit fritters and sponge fritters.

FRUIT FRITTERS

A variety of fruit may be used: quartered bananas, orange sections, halved peaches or apricots and apple rings. If using apple or pear keep them in a bowl of slightly salted water before cooking to prevent them from discolouring.

Dip the fruit in either Coating or Rich Coating Batter and fry in hot smoking fat until golden brown all over. Serve as soon as possible rolled in sugar.

CAKE OR SPONGE FRITTERS

Cut sponge cake into fingers and make a sandwich of two fingers with jam, dip them in a Rich Coating Batter, and fry in hot smoking fat.

Serve sprinkled with sugar.

YORKSHIRE PUDDING

This may be cooked in a shallow dish large enough for the number of portions or in individual small tins. For the larger tin you will need about 1 tbsp. of hot dripping from the meat.

This must be made smoking hot then add a suitable quantity of the Basic Batter and cook in a hot oven for about 40 minutes. It should rise well and be golden brown. Individual tins will take 10-15 minutes.

TOAD IN THE HOLE

300 ml. / ½ pt. Basic Batter mix
1 tbsp. dripping
225 g. / ½ lb. sausages

Heat the dripping in a shallow oven dish until smoking, add the sausages, pour on the batter and cook in a hot oven 450° F. / 220° C./ gas 7 for 45 minutes.

YEAST BUNS, SCONES AND BISCUITS

CHELSEA BUNS

225 g. / 8 oz. flour
Pinch of salt
115 g. / 4 oz. currants and sultanas
60 g. /2 oz. sugar
15 g. / ½ oz. yeast
120 ml. / 4 fl. oz. milk and water
30 g. / 1 oz. lard
1 egg
Little melted fat
Sugar glaze

Sieve the flour and salt. Mix the fruit with 2 tsp. of sugar. Cream the yeast with ½ tsp. of sugar and mix with the warmed liquid, add 1/3rd. of the flour and put to one side until it sets to a sponge.

Rub the fat into the rest of the flour and add the rest of the sugar; gradually beat in the egg and then the sponged mixture; beat well with the hand and put in a warm place when it will rise. When double in size knead lightly on a floured board.

Roll into an oblong, brush with the melted fat and put the fruit on top, roll this up with the hands. Cut slices about 2½ cm / 1 in. thick and place on a baking tin, leave to "prove" for 25 minutes. Bake in a hot oven 450° F. / 225° C. / gas 7 for 15-20 minutes until risen and golden brown; just before finished cooking brush with a sugar glaze made by melting sugar in hot water and boiling until syrupy.

BATH BUNS

225 g. / 8 oz. flour
Pinch of salt
90 g. / 3 oz. margarine
70 ml. /2.5 fl. oz. milk
15 g. / ½ oz. yeast
1 beaten egg
60 g. / 2 oz. sugar

60 g. / 2 oz. sultanas
30 g. / 1 oz. candied peel
egg & milk to glaze
30 g. / 1 oz. sugar

Sieve flour and salt. Warm the milk and use a little to cream the yeast, pour this with the rest of the milk into the flour, add the beaten egg and beat well with the hands, cover with a cloth and leave to rise in a warm place until it is double in size (about 1½ hours).

Add sugar and fruit, beat well and form into small balls. Put on greased baking tin and leave to "prove" until they have doubled their size; brush with the egg and milk, sprinkle with sugar and bake in hot oven 450° F. / 225° C. / gas 7 for about 25 minutes.

DOUGHNUTS

Make the dough as for Bath Buns, when it has risen knead lightly, divide into 12 pieces, shape each into a ball, flatten a bit and put ¼ tsp. of jam in the centre, then gather the edges together over the jam, place on a greased, floured tin and leave in a warm place for about 10 minutes to "prove".

Heat some fat in a deep pan until just smoking hot and deep fry the doughnuts for about 5 minutes until they are golden brown. Drain well and dredge with sugar or sugar and cinnamon. Serve immediately.

HOT CROSS BUNS

800 g. / 1¾ lb. flour
30 g. / 1 oz. yeast
115 g. / 4 oz. sugar
425 ml. / ¾ pt. warm milk
pinch of salt
¼ tsp. ground cinnamon
¼ tsp. grated nutmeg
120 g. / 5 oz. currants
30 g. / 1 oz. candied peel
115 g. / 4 oz. butter
2 beaten eggs
Milk and sugar glaze

Sieve 225 g. / ½ lb. of flour; cream the yeast with a little sugar and stir in the milk, add to the sieved flour and mix well. Cover with a cloth and leave in a warm place to set the sponge about 20 minutes. Sieve the rest of the flour and add the sugar, salt, cinnamon, nutmeg, currants and peel, mix well. Melt the fat and beat in the eggs.

Stir all the dry ingredients into the "sponge" and pour in the fat and eggs, mix well beating with the hands, cover and leave in a warm place to rise to double its size, about 1 hour.

Flour the hands and form the dough into round buns, place them on a greased floured baking tin, cut a cross on the top and leave in a warm place for about 25 minutes to "prove". It may be necessary to re-mark the cross before baking in a hot oven 450° F. / 225° C. / gas 7 for about 15 minutes.

When almost cooked brush them with the glaze.

SCONES

225 g. / 8 oz. flour
pinch of salt
1 tsp. cream of tartar
½ tsp. bicarbonate of soda
60 g. / 2 oz. fat
150 ml. / ¼ pt. milk

Sieve the flour, salt, cream of tartar and bicarbonate; and rub in the fat. Make a well in the centre and mix in enough milk to make a spongy dough just firm enough to handle.

Put onto a floured board and roll out lightly to 2½ cm / 1 in. thick, cut rounds with a floured cutter, place on a floured baking tin and cook in a hot oven 450° F. / 225° C. / gas 7 for about 8 minutes until brown and well risen.

The scones may be glazed with beaten egg and milk before cooking

FRUIT SCONES
Add 60 g. / 2 oz. currants, sultanas or raisins to the dry ingredients.

OATMEAL SCONES
Replace 60 g. / 2 oz. of the flour with the same quantity of oatmeal.

RICH TEA SCONES

Add 2 tbsp. of sugar to the dry ingredients and use 1 beaten egg with 2 tbsp. of milk for the mixing. Again fruit may be added.

GARIBALDI BISCUITS

60 g. / 2 oz. currants
115 g. / 4 oz. flour
pinch of salt
30 g. / 1 oz. butter
30 g. / 1 oz. sugar
milk to mix

Rub the butter into the flour and salt with the fingertips, then stir in the sugar, add enough milk to make a stiff dough. Roll out on a floured board about 3 mm / 1/8 in. thick, keep the dough regular in shape; cut it in half, sprinkle one half evenly with chopped fruit and cover with the other half.

Roll again until it returns to the original thickness, keeping it as regular as possible. Trim the edges and cut into squares, bake on a greased tin 400° F. / 200° C. / gas 6 for about 15 minutes.

DIGESTIVE BISCUITS

180 g. / 6 oz. flour
Pinch of salt
45 g. / 1½ oz. coarse oatmeal
30 g. / 1 oz. sugar
90 g. / 3 oz. lard or fat
Milk to mix

Mix the dry ingredients and rub in the fat , mix in enough milk to make a firm dough. Roll out on a floured board thinly and cut into rounds with a floured cutter.

Prick the surface with a fork , place on a greased baking tin and cook at 400° F. / 200° C. / gas 6 for about 15 minutes until lightly coloured.

SHORTBREAD

180 g. / 6 oz. flour
Pinch of salt
115 g. / 4 oz. butter
60 g. / 2 oz. sugar

Sieve the flour and the salt and rub in the fat, add the sugar and knead until the mixture binds together. Roll out on a floured board and form into a round cake, crimp the edges, prick the surface with a fork and score into wedges.

Place on a baking tin lined with greased paper and bake at 325° F./ 160° C./ gas 4 for about 1 hour until lightly brown, cool and sprinkle with sugar.

GINGER SHORTBREAD

Simply add ½ tsp. ground ginger and 30 g. / 1 oz. finely chopped ginger to the Shortbread mix.

CAKES

Although the cooking times and oven temperature is given in individual recipes the exact time depends on the consistency of the mixture, its position in the oven and the depth of the cake.

As a general rule small cakes or buns and sponge cakes are put near the top of the oven and large cakes in the centre.

A cake which is to be cooked for several hours will require covering after about 2 hours with greaseproof paper to prevent it over browning.

When a cake is cooked it should be well risen and golden brown but the best test is to push a hot skewer into the centre of the cake, it should come out clean with none of the cake mixture sticking to it. Always allow the cake to cool slightly before taking it out of the tin, turn out gently and place on a cake rack until quite cold, then store in an airtight tin. Fruit cakes and gingerbreads should be kept for at least 24 hours whilst rich fruit cakes improve with longer.

PLAIN FRUIT CAKE

225 g. / 8 oz. flour
pinch of salt
115 g. / 4 oz. margarine
90 g. / 3 oz. sugar
¼ tsp. mixed spice
115 g. / 4 oz. dried fruit
Grated rind of a lemon
1 beaten egg
Milk to mix

Sieve the flour and salt and rub in the fat with the finger tips until mixture is like breadcrumbs, add sugar, spice, fruit and lemon rind and mix with the egg and milk to give a dropping consistency, it should drop off a spoon in about 5 seconds.

Put mixture in a well greased 150 cm / 6 in. cake tin and bake in centre of oven at 350° F. / 175° C. / gas 4 for about 1¼ hours.

The same mixture can be used for buns but with a stiffer consistency, these should be baked near the top of the oven at 450° F. / 220° C. / gas 7 for 15-20 minutes.

ROCK CAKES

360 g. / 12 oz. flour
Pinch of salt
¼ tsp. grated nutmeg
¼ tsp. mixed spice
180 g. / 6 oz. margarine
150 g. / 5 oz. sugar
90 g. / 3 oz. currants
45 g. / 1½ oz. candied peel finely chopped
1 beaten egg and milk to mix

Make the cake mixture as for the Fruit Cake, but fairly stiff. Grease a baking sheet and lightly flour it; place the mixture in small heaps on the sheet and bake near the top of the oven at 450° F. / 220° C. / gas 7 for 15-20 minutes.

PLAIN CHERRY CAKE

225 g. / 8 oz. flour
115 g. / 4 oz. margarine
115 g. / 4 oz. sugar
2 beaten eggs
60 g. / 2 oz. glace cherries cut in half
grated rind of a lemon
milk to mix

Sieve the flour and rub in the fat, add the sugar and eggs, now add most of the cherries and lemon rind and mix with the milk to a dropping consistency.

Put in a greased cake tin, place the rest of the cherries on top and dredge a little sugar over. Cook in the centre of the oven at 375° F. / 190° C. / gas 6 for about 1½ hours.

FARMHOUSE FRUIT CAKE

225 g. / 8 oz. wholemeal flour
225 g. / 8 oz. self raising flour
½ tsp. mixed spice
½ tsp bicarb. of soda
180 g. / 6 oz. dripping
180 g. / 6 oz. sugar
225 g. / 8 oz. dried fruit
30 g. / 1 oz. chopped candied peel
2 beaten eggs and milk to mix

Sieve the flours, spice and bicarbonate and rub in the fat; add the sugar, fruit and peel then mix with eggs and milk to a fairly soft consistency. Put into a greased cake tin and cook at 400 F. / 200 C. / gas 7 for about 2 hours.

SPONGE CAKES

Sponge cake mixtures contain little or no fat and follow a different mixing technique. The eggs and sugar are put in a large basin over a pan of hot water and whisked until thick enough to retain the impression of the whisk; the basin is then removed from the heat and the flour folded in very lightly using a metal spoon; it must **NOT** be beaten, the idea is to keep all the air that has been whisked in.

The whisking is **VERY IMPORTANT** and must not be skimped it will take about 20 minutes.

SPONGE LAYER CAKE

4 eggs
115 g. / 4 oz. sugar
100 g. / 3½ oz. flour
30 g. / 1 oz. melted butter
jam

Make the sponge mix and then fold in the melted butter which must not be too hot. Pour the mixture into a greased 180 cm / 7 in. cake tin and bake at 350 F. / 175 C. / gas 4 for about 1 hour.

When the cake is cold slice in half, fill with jam and sandwich together.

ORANGE or LEMON SPONGE LAYER CAKE

Make as for Sponge Layer but add some finely grated orange or lemon rind. When cold sandwich with orange or lemon butter icing. It can then be covered with orange or lemon glace icing.

YULETIDE LOG

3 eggs
90 g. / 3 oz. sugar
60 g. / 2 oz. grated chocolate or chocolate powder
1 tbsp. hot water
1 tbsp. milk
90 g. / 3 oz. flour
Chocolate butter icing

Whisk the eggs and sugar as normal and add the chocolate dissolved in the hot water and add the milk, then fold in the flour.

Take a baking tin about 30 x 23 cm / 12 x 9 in. and grease it, next line it with greaseproof paper and grease this paper as well.

Pour the mixture into the tin and cook at 475 F. / 240 C. / gas 9 for about 8 minutes. Turn it out onto sugared greaseproof paper and roll it up.

When cold unroll it and spread with the chocolate butter icing, roll it up again and cover the outside with more of the icing, mark the surface of the icing to look like a log, a dusting of icing sugar will give the appearance of frost; add a sprig of holly.

GINGERBREADS

450 g. / 1 lb. flour
½ tsp. salt
1½ tsp ground ginger
½ tsp. bicarb. of soda
225 g. / 8 oz. brown sugar
180 g. / 6 oz. margarine

340 g. / ¾ lb. treacle or golden syrup
300 ml. / ½ pt. milk
1 beaten egg

Sieve all the dry ingredients together, warm the sugar and treacle together but not too hot, warm the milk and the beaten egg; mix everything together.

Grease a shallow straight sided baking tin, line with greaseproof paper and grease the paper; pour in the mixture and bake at 350° F. / 175° C. / gas 4 for about 1½ hours, turn out and leave until cold, then cut the cake into squares or fingers.

RICH CAKES

This is probably the biggest group of cakes and always follows the same method of mixing.

The fat and the sugar are creamed together either with a wooden spoon or an electric mixer, then the beaten eggs are added one at a time the mixture being well beaten all the time, it is important that a very thorough beating is carried out at this stage. Then the dry ingredients are added being mixed in thoroughly but **NOT** beaten. Sufficient liquid should be added to give a soft dropping consistency i.e., the mixture should drop off the mixing spoon without having to shake it.

The cake tin should be well greased and then lined with greased greaseproof paper. The tin should only be ¾ filled and the top of the mixture levelled off; if the cake is to be iced a slight hollow should be formed in the top of the mixture so that it will end up level after cooking.

Because these cakes are usually baked for a long time it is necessary to cover them with a double layer of greaseproof paper towards the end of the cooking time to prevent them from becoming overbrown.

RICH FRUIT CAKE
This is the cake which is used for Christmas Cakes etc.

450 g. / 1 lb. currants
225 g. / 8 oz. seedless raisins
450 g. / 1 lb. sultanas

180 g. / 6 oz. mixed peel
115 g. / 4 oz. glace cherries
115 g. / 4 oz. chopped almonds
300 g. / 10 oz. margarine
300 g. / 10 oz. sugar
8 eggs
350 g. / 12 oz. flour
Pinch of salt
2 tsp. mixed spice
Grated rind of a lemon
Squeeze of lemon juice
Milk or brandy

Cream the fat and sugar and add the eggs; sieve the dry ingredients into a mixing bowl and add the fruit, peel, chopped cherries, almonds and lemon rind, mix thoroughly then gradually fold in the creamed mix.

Continue to mix lightly adding the lemon juice and the milk or brandy to get the right consistency. Put the mixture into a prepared 23 cm / 9 in. cake tin and bake at 350 F. / 175 C. / gas 4 for 2 hours, then lower the temperature to 300° F. / 150° C. / gas 1 for a further 2½-3 hours.

For Christmas Cakes etc. this cake is finished with Almond Paste and Royal Icing.

MADEIRA CAKE

225 g. / 8 oz. flour
pinch of salt
little grated lemon rind
150 g. / 5 oz. sugar
150 g. / 5 oz. butter
3 eggs
Few drops of lemon essence
Milk to mix

Cream the sugar and fat, then fold in the sieved dry ingredients and add the lemon essence and milk as required. Put the mixture into a prepared cake tin and bake at 375° F. / 190° C. / gas 6 for about 1¼ hours.

DUNDEE CAKE

180 g. / 6 oz. sultanas
90 g. / 3 oz. currants
60 g. / 2 oz. candied orange peel
60 g. / 2 oz. chopped almonds
250 g. / 9 oz. flour
Pinch of salt
180 g. / 6 oz. butter
180 g. / 6 oz. sugar
3 eggs
Milk to mix
15 g. / ½ oz. whole almonds

Cream the fat and sugar and beat in the eggs; then fold in the dry ingredients except the whole almonds, mix with sufficient milk to the right consistency and put in a prepared cake tin, place the whole almonds on the top; bake at 350° F. / 175° C. / gas 4 for 1½-2 hours.

VICTORIA SANDWICH CAKE

115 g. / 4 oz. butter
115 g. / 4 oz. sugar
2 eggs
115 g. / 4 oz. flour
Milk to mix
Jam

Cream the fat and sugar and beat in the eggs, then fold in the flour and add sufficient milk, put into two greased and lined sandwich tins and bake at 375° F. / 190° C. / gas 6 for 25-30 mins. When cold, sandwich with the jam and dust with a little sugar.

CHOCOLATE VICTORIA SANDWICH CAKE

Make as the Plain cake but replace 1 tbsp. of flour with 1 tbsp. of cocoa. This sandwich can be filled with plain or chocolate butter icing.

CAKE FILLINGS AND ICINGS

BUTTER ICING

Very effective if the colour contrasts with the colour of the biscuits or cakes; can also be used as a soft cake covering.

90 g. / 3 oz. butter
115 g. / 4 oz. icing sugar
Vanilla essence
Colouring if needed

Cream the fat then add the sieved sugar gradually and beat until smooth and creamy, then add a few drops of vanilla essence and the colouring.

ORANGE or LEMON BUTTER ICING

Add finely grated orange or lemon rind and a little of the fruit juice to the Butter Icing.

COFFEE BUTTER ICING

Leave out the vanilla essence in the Butter Icing and beat in coffee essence to taste.

CHOCOLATE BUTTER ICING

Make the Butter Icing and instead of the colouring use 45 g. / 1½ oz. of chocolate powder or the same quantity of melted chocolate.

COFFEE WALNUT CREAM

Make Coffee Butter Icing and add 2 tbsp. of finely chopped walnuts. Almonds or other nuts can be used.

ALMOND FILLING

2 tbsp. ground almonds
2 tbsp. apricot jam
1 tsp. vanilla essence
1 tbsp. thick cream

Mix all the ingredients together until well mixed.

BANANA CREAM FILLING

2-3 bananas
60 g. / 2 oz. sugar
1 tsp. grated lemon rind
2 tbsp. cream

Mash the bananas into a pulp, beat in the lemon rind and the sugar and fold in the stiffly beaten cream.

RASPBERRY or STRAWBERRY FILLING

115 g. / 4 oz. fruit pulped
4 tbsp. cream
60 g. / 2 oz. sugar
2 tbsp. cake crumbs

Mash the fruit and the sugar with a fork add the sieved crumbs and fold in the cream.

GLACE ICING

This is a soft icing easy to make and as it does not harden is suitable for small cakes, biscuits etc.

Basic recipe
225 g. / 8 oz. sieved icing sugar
3 tbsp. warm water
Flavouring and colouring as required

Put the icing sugar, water and flavouring into a small pan and gently heat, stirring, until mixture is warm and sugar dissolved. Do NOT make it too hot, it should coat the back of a wooden spoon evenly and look smooth and glossy.

Colour as necessary and use immediately. Stand the cake etc. to be iced on a wire dray with a plate underneath and pour the warm icing over, it should flow smoothly over the top and run slowly down coating the sides.

The consistency of the icing is critical, if it is too thick it will not flow smoothly over the cake, if it is too thin it will run off leaving too thin a coating. Always check with the wooden spoon method before using; if it is too thin add a little more icing sugar, if it is too thick add a few drops of warm water.

CHOCOLATE GLACE ICING

60 g. / 2 oz. grated chocolate
2 tbsp. warm water
225 g. / 8 oz. sieved icing sugar
2 tsp. vanilla essence

Melt the chocolate in the warm water over a low heat, let it cool then add the icing sugar and essence again over a low heat until sugar is dissolved, do NOT let it get too hot.

Chocolate powder may be used in place of grated chocolate.

COFFEE GLACE ICING

Use the basic recipe but with 2 tbsp. of warm water and coffee essence to taste.

ORANGE or LEMON GLACE ICING

Use the basic recipe but substitute the appropriate fruit juice for the water and add the appropriate colouring.

ROYAL ICING

900 g. / 2 lb. sieved icing sugar
4 egg whites
colouring if required

Make a well in the centre of the icing sugar and gradually add the lightly beaten egg whites, keep stirring and only add enough of the egg whites to give a stiff but beatable mixture. Any colouring should be added carefully drop by drop and well beaten in. Beat the mixture thoroughly until it is smooth and glossy. This quantity will cover a 230 cm / 10 in. cake, and is used on rich cakes such as Birthday and Christmas. Before covering with Royal Icing these cakes have a coating of Almond Icing.

ALMOND ICING

225 g. / 1 lb. sieved icing sugar
225 g. / 1 lb. ground almonds
2 lightly beaten eggs
1 tsp. vanilla essence
Juice of a lemon

Mix the icing sugar and almonds, then add the other ingredients, stir and mix to a stiff paste, knead well.

A packaged substitute for this icing is sold as MARZIPAN which is used in the same way.

COVERING A CAKE

The cake should be a good shape, if it has risen unevenly trim it a little, if it slightly overbrown rub it gently with a grater and remove any loose crumbs. It is usual to cover top and sides of these rich cakes. First brush the surface with slightly beaten egg white or warm sieved apricot jam.

Roll out about half of the Almond Icing into a round the size of the cake top, place the icing on and lightly roll, measure the circumference of the cake and roll out two strips, each long enough to go halfway around and the same width as the height of the cake, place the strips on the cake brush the join with egg white; smooth the sides by rolling a straight sided jam jar round it.

Cover the cake and leave in a warm dry place for a week before applying the Royal Icing.

The Royal Icing should be stiff enough to stand up in points in the basin.

Stand the cake on a plate over a basin to facilitate turning; have a jug of boiling water and a palette knife ready.

Put about half the icing on the top of the cake and level it roughly, then cover the sides in the same way. Use the palette knife to smooth the surface dipping the blade in the hot water frequently using long strokes.

To create a "snow scene" finish wait until the icing starts to harden about 1 hour, then using a knife or a fork work the surface up into points.

Before attempting to decorate the icing the cake must be left in a warm place covered with greaseproof paper for several days so that the icing may dry. Decoration or piping is done with a series of nozzles which may be purchased as a set with instructions for use.

IF YOU HAVE NOT DONE ANY PIPING BEFORE, IT IS A GOOD IDEA TO PRACTICE ON A PLATE BEFORE ATTEMPTING THE CAKE.

DESSERTS

CHOCOLATE AND PEAR CRUMBLE

4 pears (not too ripe)
4 plums (not too ripe)
50 ml. / 2 fl. oz. dry cider or white wine
50 g. / 2 oz. butter
115 g. / 4 oz. flour
30 g. / 1 oz. sugar
60 g. / 2 oz. grated or chopped milk chocolate

Peel, core and chop the pears into dice; peel, quarter and stone the plums. Put the fruit in a pan with the cider, bring to the boil and simmer for about 5 minutes to soften the fruit. Make the crumble by rubbing the fat into the flour and sugar until it looks like breadcrumbs, stir in the chocolate.

Put the fruit into an ovenproof dish and cover with the crumble, cook at 400 F. / 200 C. / gas 6 until golden brown, about 20 minutes.

UPSIDE DOWN PEAR PUDDING

2 pears
200 g. / 7 oz. butter
75 g. / 3 oz. Demerara sugar
2 tbsp. golden syrup
180 g. / 6 oz. sugar
3 eggs, separated
Grated rind and juice of a lemon
150 g. / 5 oz. flour

Peel the pears, cut in half and scoop out the core, cut into slices lengthwise and simmer gently until tender. Melt 30 g. / 1 oz. of the butter in a pan with the Demerara sugar and golden syrup and cook over a low heat until the sugar has just dissolved pour this over the bottom and sides of a 1½ l / 2½ pt. pudding basin, when this caramel mix begins to set arrange the pear slices around the side of the basin, sticking them to the caramel, also put some on the bottom.

Now beat the rest of the butter with the sugar until fluffy, beat in the egg yolks and lemon rind, then fold in the flour and lemon juice. Whisk the egg whites until stiff and fold in. Pour this into the basin smooth the top with a knife and bake at 325° F. / 170° C. / gas 3 for 50 minutes.

Turn out onto a serving plate and serve hot with fresh cream.

CARAMEL ORANGES

4 large oranges
175 g. / 6 oz. soft brown sugar
200 ml. / 7 fl. oz. water
1 tbsp. Kirsch

Peel one orange very thinly and cut this peel into thin, matchstick strips, boil in water for 5 minutes, drain and reserve.

Peel the rest of the oranges and carefully remove the pith from all 4. Slice the oranges horizontally, secure the slices of each orange together with a cocktail stick.

Make a syrup by dissolving the sugar in half the water, boil until it starts to turn a deep golden. Remove from the heat, stand well back from the pan and add the rest of the water, Kirsch and strips of peel; stir over a gentle heat to dissolve any lumps, pour over the oranges and leave to cool.

Serve chilled with fresh cream.

FRENCH APPLE TART

350 g. / 12 oz. Shortcrust pastry
5 apples
30 g. / 1 oz. sugar
60 g. / 2 oz. melted butter
3 tbsp apricot jam (no lumps)
1 tbsp. Kirsch

Grease a 30 cm. / 12 in. ovenproof plate and cover with the pastry. Peel the apples, remove the cores and cut in half lengthwise. Place the halves on a board and slice them thinly.

Chop any broken or small pieces of apple and pile in the centre of the pastry. Now starting about 2½ cm / 1 in. from the outside edge of the plate arrange the apple slices in circles over lapping them slightly row by row working towards the centre.

Fold the pastry edge over to make a rim around the apples, sprinkle with sugar and drip over the melted butter, cook at 400 F. / 200 C. / gas 6 for 45 minutes or until top is golden; melt the jam with the Kirsch and brush this over the apples, cook for another 5-10 minutes until slightly caramelised.

APRICOT BAKEWELL TART

375 g. / 13 oz. shortcrust pastry
2 tbsp. apricot jam
400 g. / 14 oz. drained tin of apricot halves
40 g. / 1½ oz. halved glace cherries
115 g. / 4 oz. butter
115 g. / 4 oz. sugar
2 eggs
30 g. / 1 oz. flour
60 g. / 2 oz. ground almonds
Grated rind of a lemon
Pinch of ground cinnamon
2 tbsp. milk
30 g. / 1 oz. flaked almonds

Roll out the pastry and use it to line a 23 cm. / 9 in. flan tin, spread the jam on the pastry base. Dry the apricot halves on kitchen paper, put a half cherry in each then place open side down on the jam, cover the whole of the base in this way.

Cream the butter and sugar together until fluffy, beat in the eggs, then fold in the sieved flour, the ground almonds, lemon rind, cinnamon and milk. Spoon this mixture into the pastry case, smooth the top and sprinkle on the almond flakes.

Cook at 400° F. / 200° C. / gas 6 for 20 minutes then reduce temperature to 350° F. / 180° C. / gas 4 for another 1½ hours.

CARIBBEAN BANANAS

4 large bananas
Grated rind and juice of an orange
Pinch of grated nutmeg
¼ tsp. ground cinnamon
3 tbsp. soft brown sugar
75 ml / 3 fl. oz. dark rum
15 g. / ½ oz. melted butter

Peel the bananas and slice them thickly on the diagonal. Lay them in a single layer in a shallow oven dish.

Mix all the other ingredients together and pour over the bananas and cook at 375° F. / 190° C. / gas 5 for 10 minutes.

Serve hot with cream.

APPLE CRUMBLE

675 g. / 1½ lb. apples
115 g. / 4 oz. brown sugar
Little grated lemon rind
90 g. / 3 oz. butter
180 g. / 6 oz. flour
90 g. / 3 oz. sugar
¼ tsp. ground ginger

Peel, core and slice the apples and cook in a little water with the brown sugar and lemon rind until soft. Place in a greased oven dish.

Rub the fat into the flour until like breadcrumbs, add the castor sugar and cinnamon and sprinkle over the apples, press down lightly

Bake at 350° F. / 180° C. / gas 4 for 35 minutes until golden.

Raspberries, rhubarb, plums or gooseberries may be used instead of the apples.

APPLE DUMPLINGS

350 g. / 12 oz. shortcrust pastry
6 large cooking apples
60 g. / 2 oz. brown sugar
Little grated lemon rind
12 cloves

Roll out the pastry and cut into 6 rounds. Peel and core the apples and place one in the centre of each round of pastry. Press the cloves in the centre of the apples and fill the core cavity with a mixture of the sugar and lemon rind. Work the pastry up and over the apples sealing the edges with a little milk, brush over with a little milk or beaten egg, dredge with castor sugar and bake on a greased baking tin at 400° F. / 200° C. / gas 6 for 30 minutes.

APPLE PUDDING

1 kg. / 2 lb. cooking apples
180 g. / 6 oz. sugar
60 g. / 2 oz. butter
2 beaten eggs
115 g. / 4 oz. breadcrumbs

Peel, core and slice the apples and cook in a little water until soft, stir in the sugar, butter and eggs. Butter the bottom and sides of pie dish and coat thickly with a layer of breadcrumbs; put in the apple pulp and cover with more breadcrumbs, put a few flakes of butter on top and bake at 350° F. / 180° C. / gas 4 for ¾ hour.

INDEX